THE SCIENCE OF CLIMATE CHANGE:

A HANDS-ON COURSE

Written by Blair H. Lee, M.S.

Illustrated by Alina Bachmann

www.SecularEclecticAcademic.com

Copyright © 2017 by Blair Lee
ISBN: 978-1-947473-01-0

First Printed 2017

Second Edition Published 2018

Update Published 2020

All rights reserved under the International
and Pan-American Copyright Conventions.

Thank you for purchasing *The Science of Climate Change: A Hands-On Course*. No part of this work may be reproduced or used in any form by any means—graphic, electronic, or mechanical including photocopying, recording, taping,or information storage and retrieval systems—without written permission from contact@ seculareclecticacademic.com.

If you purchased an ebook, in order to avoid any copyright infringements of this book, please do not share (email, download, print and distribute, resale, etc.) any portion of this book to anyone outside your immediate family and for any use other than with your own children.

Note: The purchaser of this book is expressly given permission to copy any pages of this book for use within his/her own family and with his/her own children.

TABLE OF CONTENTS

Introduction 5

Climate Change: in Four Parts 6

Part 1: The Greenhouse Effect 7
First Things First: Air 7
    How Many Molecules Are in a Box of Air 9
Air Is a Mixture of Different Kinds of Gas Molecules 12
    How Small Amounts Can Have a Big Effect 13
Molecules Can Absorb the Sun's Energy 15
    Absorbing the Sun's Energy 16
Greenhouse Gases 17
    How Many Molecules Are in a Box of Air, Continued 18
    Vibrating Molecules Heat Things Up: The Greenhouse Effect 19

Part 2: Global Warming 23
Too Much of a Good Thing: Global Warming 23
    Machine-Made or Not 24
Making Energy: The Combustion Reaction 25
    In the Name of Science: An Activity Where You Generate Greenhouse Gases 26
    Time for Some Math: How Many More? 27
How Do Scientists Know the Concentration of Greenhouse Gases in the Air? 28
    Graph the Concentrations of Greenhouse Gases 29
Feedback Mechanisms 37
    Make a Positive Feedback Loop for Methane 39

Part 3: Climate Change 41
First a Word about the Weather 41
    The Weather 41
    The Climate: What Has the Weather Been at My House for the Past 30 Years? 43
The Evidence for Climate Change 46
    Melting Sea Ice Coloring Activity 49
    The Effect of the Rising Temperature on a Major Carbon Sink: Sinking Time into the Scientific Method 50
What Does It Matter if the Temperature Rises a Little? 53
    Adaptation Activity: It's All about the Rate 55

Part 4: What Can Be Done to Help? 57
Alternative Sources of Energy 57
    Comparing the Carbon "Tire"-Prints of Cars Activity 58
Your Carbon Footprint and How You Can Reduce It 59
    Food Has a Carbon Footprint: Field Trip to the Grocery Store 60
    Why Recycle? 63
    How I Am Going to Shrink My Carbon Footprint 65
    What We Can Do to Solve It Poster 67

Bibliography 69

List of Supplies 70

Appendix 1: How Many Molecules Are in a Box of Air Template 71

Appendix 2: Graph the Concentrations of Greenhouse Gases 73

Appendix 3: Field Trip to the Grocery Store Worksheet 75

Appendix 4: Answer Key 77

Glossary 90

This book is dedicated to the planet Earth.
You have always provided for us so well.
It is time for us to return the favor.

I owe many thanks to the people who helped with this book. Special thanks go to the following people for their help and support: The Wapniarski Girls, Arlene de Anda, and Meghan O'Leary

To my reviewers, I thank you so much! This book is far better because of your input. Thank you to Valerie Grosso, Kate Johnson, Kat Hutcheson, Rachel Cunningham Durand, Christina Keller, Jim Lee, and Alexandra Sommers. I want to especially thank the three student reviewers, Logan Chungo, Owen Keller, and Sean Lee. We are counting on kids, like you, to get us out of this mess!

Thank you to the scientists who are working to better understand and solve this current environmental crisis. I particularly want to thank Ed Dlugokencky from the National Oceanic and Atmospheric Administration (NOAA) for answering every one of my questions, even on the weekends, and helping me so that the concentration data is up-to-date as of the printing of this book.

INTRODUCTION

The world is in the middle of an environmental crisis. This crisis has become even worse since I wrote this book in 2017. A critical step to solving this crisis is to understand the science explaining it, the science of global warming and climate change. The content in *The Science of Climate Change: A Hands-On Course* has been structured so that it begins with the basics, the foundational fundamentals, needed to understand global warming and climate change and builds from these basics.

The science explaining global warming and climate change is not complicated. There are several concepts from different science disciplines that need to be brought together, however, to have a solid understanding of these two interrelated topics. I worked hard to ensure that readers have a clear explanation of these concepts, showing where they connect and intersect, to ensure they will have a solid understanding of global warming and climate change.

Throughout *The Science of Climate Change: A Hands-On Course*, students are encouraged to interact with the text. Space is provided to answer questions, to create their own graphs showing important trends, and even to color illustrations. Interacting with academic material in this way draws attention to important concepts. This helps students remain engaged and thus gain ownership over the material. The material then becomes knowledge that he or she can possess, which builds in future science courses.

Often the language in the course is conversational and casual. This is not a typical style for a science course. I am a retired college professor, and I write science material as if I were conversing with students in person. My style as a teacher was not formal and neither is my style as a writer. I believe that science topics presented this way are more approachable. It distresses me when I hear people say, "Science is too hard. I am not good at it." I believe that science is not too hard for anyone, and that everyone can be "good" at science. I feel that presenting material in a more casual manner helps with this.

Blair Lee
Parent, scientist, educator, writer, and fellow citizen

CLIMATE CHANGE: IN FOUR PARTS

This book is about climate change and the global warming causing it. You hear a lot about climate change and global warming in the news, but what do these terms mean? The weather feels the same now as it did last year. What are scientists worried about? You may have heard that polar bears are in danger of extinction because of climate change. How is that possible? If you do not understand how and why there is climate change and global warming and how these can be a problem for polar bears and other **organisms**, living beings, you are not alone.

There are several parts to understanding climate change. The science in each part is not difficult. The issue is bringing all the parts together to understand how they connect. Climate change is like one of those big puzzles that need to be put together before you can see the whole picture. Climate change is the science issue of your lifetime. For that reason, it is important to learn about it so you can understand how you can help. Polar bears are counting on you.

PART 1: THE GREENHOUSE EFFECT

First Things First: Air

Look around you. You are surrounded by something. Do you know what it is? It is not the walls or furniture. It is not trees, grass, or buildings. It is **air**. The particles that make air are so small they are invisible to your eyes. They are so small you usually cannot feel them around you. They are there though. You can prove it by breathing in and out. Why don't you do that now? Breathe in, put your hand up to your mouth, and blow the breath out onto your hand.

You might not be able to see the particles that make air, but you can feel them on your hand, can't you?

Air Is Made of Gas Molecules. The tiny particles that make air are called **molecules**. To understand climate change, you need to know something about the chemistry of molecules.

One molecule is so small you cannot see it. Many molecules must group together to make things you can see. Mountains, grassy fields, sheep, trees, and rivers are all made from huge numbers of molecules.

The molecules that make air are gas molecules. They do not group together the way those that make mountains do. Air molecules are loners that zip around running into things, including you. In fact, they are bouncing between you and this book right now!

Molecules are made from even smaller particles called atoms. There are many different kinds of **atoms**. It is the type and number of atoms in a molecule that determine what the molecule is. The types of molecules determine what is made. For example, the types of molecules that make mountains are different from those that make air or water.

A molecule of sand is made from 1 atom of silicon (Si) and 2 atoms of oxygen (O).

A molecule of water is made from 2 atoms of hydrogen (H) and 1 atom of oxygen (O).

A person is made from many different kinds of molecules. The most common types of atoms in the molecules that make people are carbon (C), hydrogen (H), oxygen (O), nitrogen (N), calcium (Ca), and phosphorus (P).

How Many Molecules Are in a Box of Air?

You are going to make a box where the length of each side is 2 **centimeters**. The box will have a volume of 8 cubic-centimeters. You will not put anything in the box. Air molecules are everywhere you are though, so your box will be full of the molecules that make air. After you make the box, you will predict the number of air molecules that are in it.

Do not turn to page 10 until after you have made the box and written your guess down.

Materials

- The How Many Molecules Are in a Box of Air Template from Appendix 1
- Scissors
- Tape (is easiest) or glue
- Pen or Pencil

Procedure

1. Make the box from the template. The instructions for making it are in Appendix 1, page 71.
2. After making the box, fill in the text box below.
3. Answer questions on the next page. Do not throw the box away. You will use it later in the course.

Before you turn the page, guess how many gas molecules are in the box.

Write your guess down here.

How Many Are There in a Box of Air? Continued

Because you cannot see air, you might think there are not many molecules in it.

There are more than **200,000,000,000,000,000,000** air molecules in the box you made!

That is a really big number. **There are a lot of molecules in a small amount of air, aren't there?** Was your guess close to this one?

A good way to handle a big number like this one is to use scientific notation. Count the number of zeros after the 2 in 200,000,000,000,000,000,000 and write it on the line to the right of and above the 10. **That is the number of molecules in 8 cubic-centimeters of air using scientific notation.**

200,000,000,000,000,000,000 = 2.0 x 10 ____

Look around the room you are in. How many boxes of air would fit in your room? Circle the best answer or fill in the blank with a guess. Try using scientific notation if you think the number is very large.

10,000 **1,000,000** **more than 1,000,000** ____________________

Walk around your house. How many boxes of air would fit in your house? Circle the best answer or fill in the blank with a guess. Try using scientific notation if you think the number is very large.

1,000,000 **100,000,000,000** **more than 100,000,000,000** ____________________

(Answers page 77.)

There are 118 different kinds of atoms listed on the **Periodic Table** (Table 1). Luckily for this discussion, air molecules are made from only a few types of atoms. Each kind of atom is listed using its abbreviation. Almost all the atoms in the air in your box are nitrogen (N), oxygen (O), argon (Ar), carbon (C), hydrogen (H), and neon (Ne).

Periodic Table

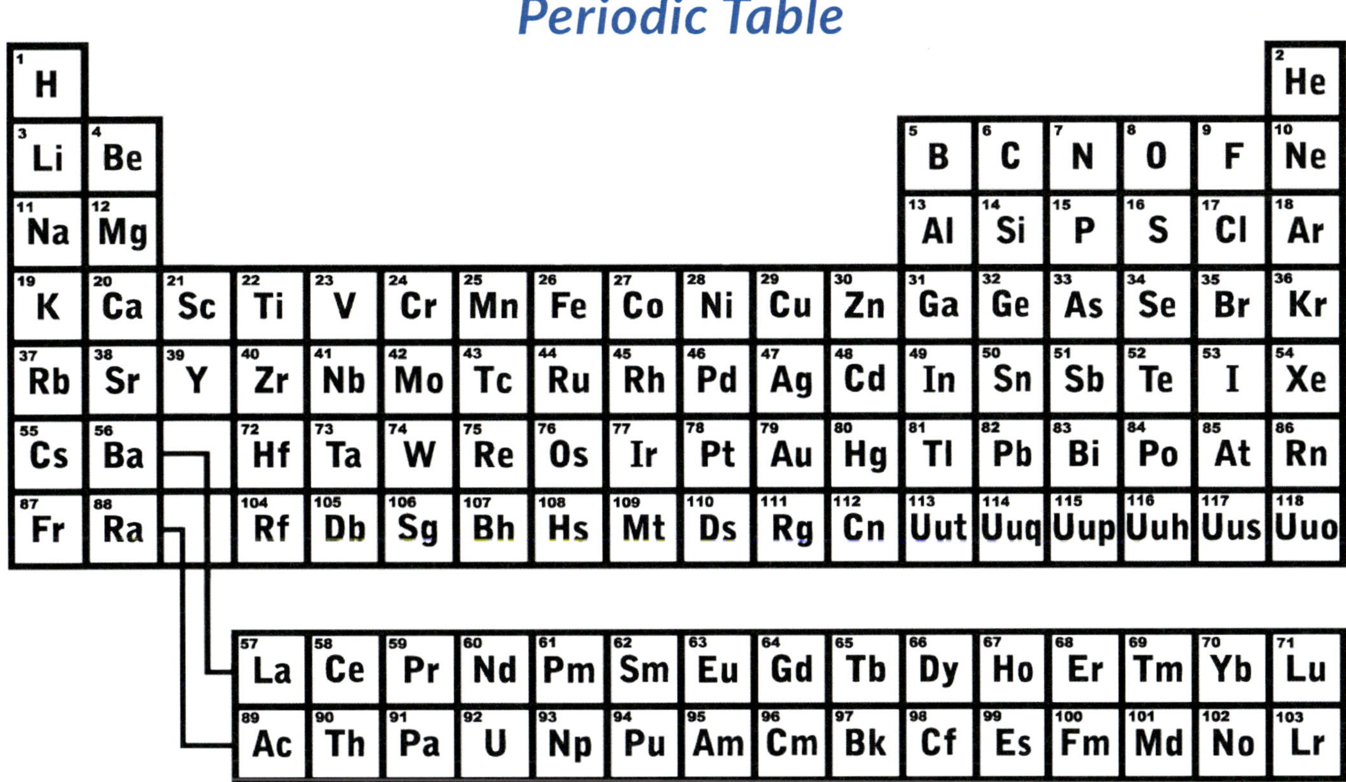

Table 1: The letters N, O, Ar, H, C, and Ne are the chemical symbols for nitrogen, oxygen, argon, hydrogen, carbon, and neon. Find and circle the six most common types of atoms that make air: N, O, Ar, H, C, and Ne. (Answers page 77.)

Some atoms, like argon and neon, float through the air all by themselves. The atoms that make nitrogen gas, oxygen gas, carbon dioxide, methane, and nitrous oxide join together to make molecules. The links between atoms where they make molecules are called bonds.

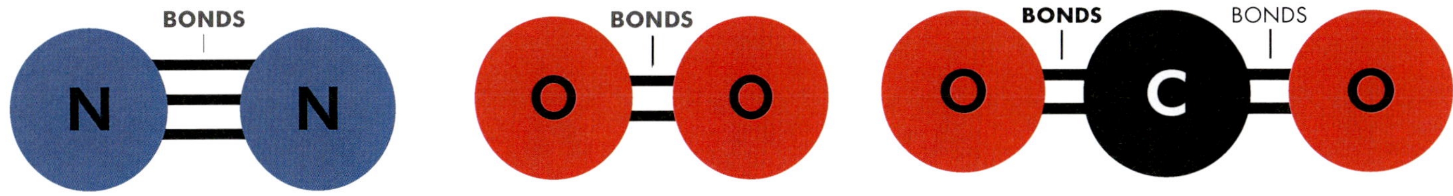

The most common molecules in air are nitrogen gas, N_2, and oxygen gas, O_2. The subscript number tells how many of the atoms are in the molecule. O_2, the molecule that makes oxygen gas, is made from two oxygen atoms bonded together. N_2O, the molecule that makes nitrous oxide, is made from two nitrogen atoms and one oxygen atom.

Concentration *is a measure of the amount of something in a mixture.*

Air is a Mixture of Different Kinds of Molecules

MOLECULE'S NAME	CHEMICAL COMPOSITION	MOLECULAR SHAPE	CONCENTRATION IN DRY AIR
NITROGEN GAS	N_2	N ≡ N	78.08%
OXYGEN GAS	O_2	O = O	20.95%
ARGON	Ar	Ar	0.93%
CARBON DIOXIDE	CO_2	O = C = O	0.0409%
NEON	Ne	Ne	0.0018%
METHANE	CH_4	H, H, C, H, H	0.0002%
NITROUS OXIDE	N_2O	N ≡ N – O	0.00005%

Table 2: These seven molecules mix together to make dry air. There are also other molecules in low concentrations in dry air.

Water vapor is in air, too. Water molecules in the gas state are called **water vapor**. The concentration of water vapor varies depending on many factors. For that reason, scientists often use measurements for dry air.

How Small Amounts Can Have a Big Effect

Is all this talk about molecules and bonds making you hot and thirsty? Why don't you make a scientific model and something to drink at the same time! As a percentage, the concentration of carbon dioxide, methane, and nitrous oxide account for a small amount of the total air molecules. Some things though, like these three molecules and drink mix flavoring and color, can have a big effect even in small concentrations. (Answers page 77.)

Materials

- 8 cups of cold water
- 1 cup ice
- Measuring cup
- 1/4 teaspoon measuring spoon
- 1 pitcher
- 1 cup sugar
- 3.6g (0.13 oz) packet unsweetened flavored drink mix, like Kool-Aid
- How Small Amounts Can Have a Big Effect Lab Sheet

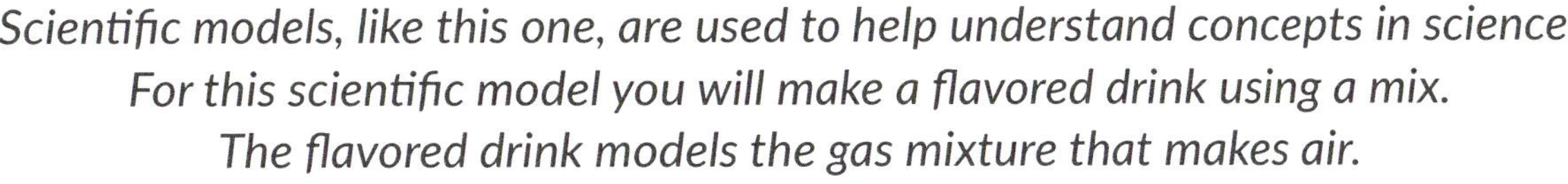

Scientific models, like this one, are used to help understand concepts in science.
For this scientific model you will make a flavored drink using a mix.
The flavored drink models the gas mixture that makes air.

The ingredients each model a component of air.

NITROGEN

OXYGEN

ARGON AND NEON

GREENHOUSE GASES

How Small Amounts Can Have a Big Effect Lab Sheet

Procedure and Observations: Follow the instruction answering the questions as you go along.

1. Pour 8 cups of water into a pitcher. Observations: How does the water taste? What color is the water? How does the water smell?

2. Measure and pour 1 cup of sugar into the pitcher. Stir until the sugar has completely dissolved into the water. Observations: Did adding the sugar to the water change the taste? Did it change the color? Does the water smell different?

3. Add the ice cubes to the sugar water mix. Observations: How did adding ice to the sugar-water mix change the taste? Did the color change? Did the smell change? The atoms argon and neon are sometimes called inert gases. What does inert mean?

4. Open the drink mix packet. Pour the contents into a **DRY** measuring cup. Observations: Based on the measurement from the cup, how much drink mix was in the packet?

5. Measure the drink mix 1/4 teaspoon at a time into the sugar water. Observations: Stir and taste after each addition. How do the taste, smell, and color change after each addition?

6. Why don't you have a drink, and think about the ingredients chosen for the model.

   Why was water chosen to model nitrogen gas?

   Why was sugar chosen to model oxygen gas?

   Why were ice cubes chosen to model argon and neon?

   Why was the drink mix chosen to model the molecules carbon dioxide, methane, and nitrous oxide? What do you think would happen if you increased the amount of drink mix?

Molecules Can Absorb The Sun's Energy

The sun's energy travels through space and heats Earth and the things on it. When you feel warmth from the sun on your skin, you are feeling heat energy.

Some molecules absorb energy from the sun and some do not.

When a molecule absorbs the sun's energy, the bonds holding the molecule together vibrate. When molecules absorb the sun's energy and vibrate they radiate, release, heat into the air. In effect, these molecules transfer the sun's energy into the air in the form of heat. This heats the air.

Trap, absorb, transfer: You will see all three of these words used to describe how energy from the sun, when it comes in contact with greenhouse gases, warms the air. It can be confusing. These words are not synonyms. How can they be used interchangeably to explain something in science?

When energy waves from the sun come in contact with greenhouse gas molecules, the bonds between the atoms of the molecules vibrate and transfer the sun's energy, in the form of heat, to the air. In effect, this traps or absorbs energy from the sun that would escape into space if greenhouse gas molecules were not present.

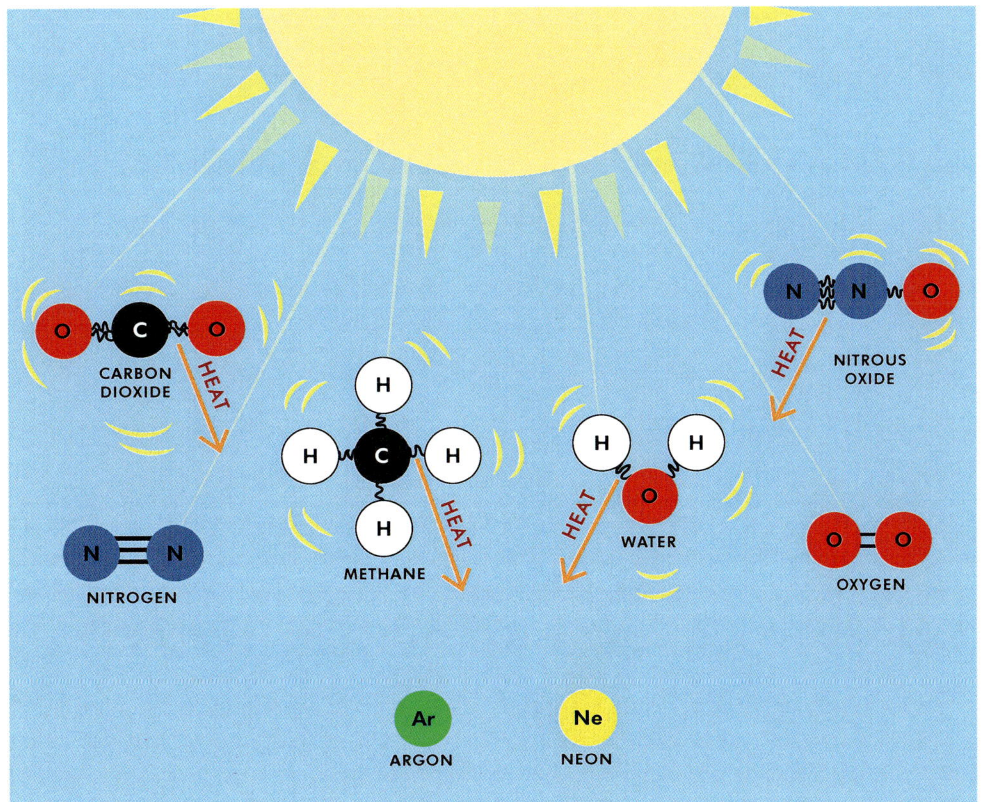

Carbon dioxide, methane, water, and nitrous oxide absorb energy from the sun and release that energy into the air in the form of heat. Nitrogen, argon, neon, and oxygen do not absorb energy from the sun and do not heat the air.

Absorbing the Sun's Energy

To understand the greenhouse effect, global warming, and climate change, it is important to have a clear understanding that molecules absorb energy from the sun and radiate the energy in the form of heat into the air. The best way to learn science is through observation. For this activity, you will observe and think about molecules absorbing energy from the sun and radiating that energy into the air in the form of heat. (Answers page 78.)

Materials: 1 piece of black construction paper, a sunny location, a timer (the one on a phone works great), and a pen or pencil.

Procedure

1. Place the black construction paper in a closed cupboard or drawer out of the sun for 30 minutes.
2. When the time is up, take it out and hold your hand about 2 ½ centimeters (1 inch) from the paper. Answer the first question.
3. Place the black construction paper outside in the sun if the day is warm or in a window with sunlight streaming through it.
4. Set the timer for 30 minutes.
5. When the timer goes off, move the paper out of the sunlight.
6. Hold your hand about 2 ½ centimeters (1 inch) from the paper. Answer the second question, and draw a diagram of the process.
7. Take the paper out of the sun. Set the timer for 5 minutes. When the timer goes off, hold your hand about 2 ½ centimeters (1 inch) from the paper. Answer the last question.

Answer the Questions

Do you feel heat radiating from the paper?

Now that the paper has been in the sunlight, do you feel more or less heat radiating from it?

The molecules in the paper absorb energy from the sun and **radiate** it as heat to your hand. Draw a quick illustration of the process that occurs at the paper. Draw the energy from the sun and the heat that radiates from the paper as waves.

Do the molecules in paper radiate more or less heat when the paper is out of direct sunlight? Why do you think that is?

Greenhouse Gases

The sun's energy is absorbed and re-radiated as heat by molecules in the air called greenhouse gas molecules. This process heats the air. **Carbon dioxide, methane, water, and nitrous oxide absorb the sun's energy and radiate it into the air; they are greenhouse gases.** Most gas molecules in air don't absorb the sun's energy. Nitrogen, oxygen, argon, and neon do not; they are not greenhouse gas molecules.

Greenhouse Gas molecules absorb and re-radiate the sun's energy. This warms air on Earth.

Greenhouse Gases

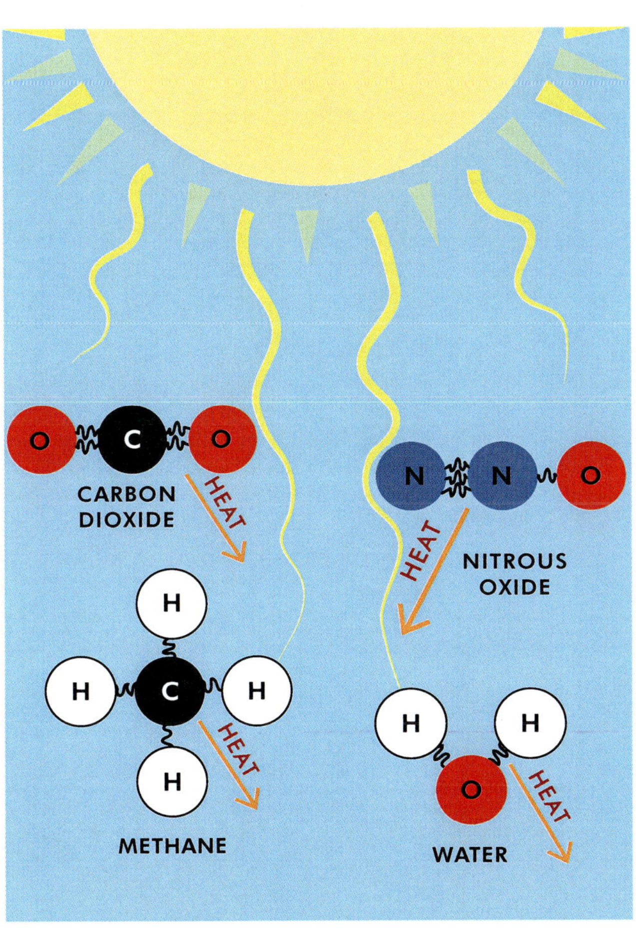

Greenhouse gases absorb and re-radiate energy from the sun into the air as heat.

Not Greenhouse Gases

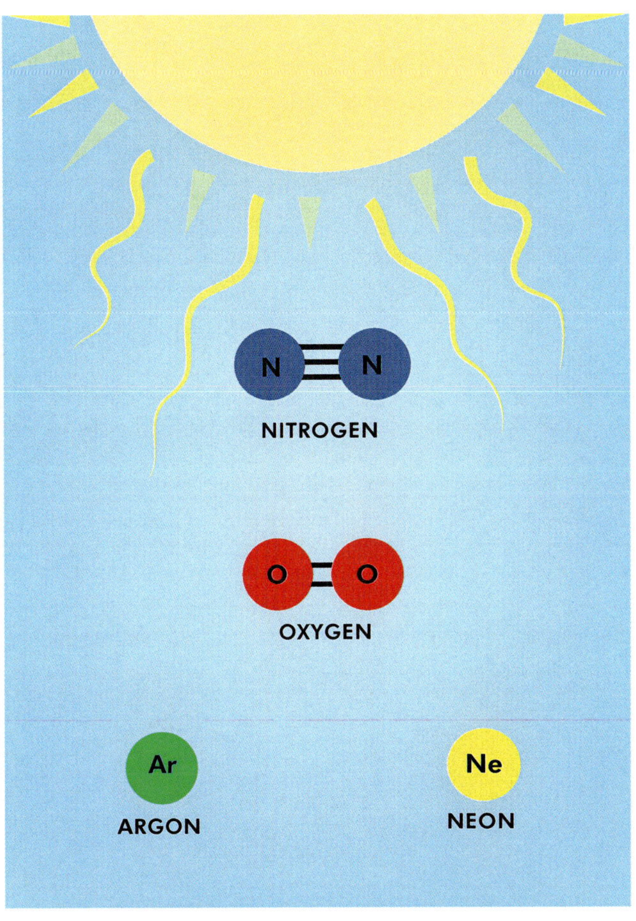

These gases do not absorb energy from the sun or heat the air.

The greenhouse gas molecules carbon dioxide, methane, and nitrous oxide exist in air in much lower concentrations than do oxygen and nitrogen. **A small sample of air, however, contains so many molecules that even in low concentrations there are a huge number of greenhouse gas molecules in the sample**.

How Many Molecules Are in a Box of Air? Continued

Put the box of air in front of you as you go over the concentration numbers in Table 3, below. There are about 2.0×10^{20} molecules in the box. On the line to the right of and above the 10, write the number that gives the correct value for each gas molecule using scientific notation.

How Many Molecules Are in Eight Cubic Centimeters of Dry Air	Chemical Formula
157,800,000,000,000,000,000 (1.578×10^{___}) nitrogen gas molecules	**N_2**
41,880,000,000,000,000,000 (4.168×10^{___}) oxygen gas molecules	**O_2**
1,860,000,000,000,000,000 (1.86×10^{___}) argon gas molecules	**Ar**
81,800,000,000,000,000 (8.18×10^{___}) carbon dioxide gas molecules	**CO_2**
3,600,000,000,000,000 (3.6×10^{___}) neon gas molecules	**Ne**
372,600,000,000,000 (3.726×10^{___}) methane gas molecules	**CH_4**
66,400,000,000,000 (6.64×10^{___}) nitrous oxide gas molecules	**N_2O**

Table 3: Seven Types of Gas Molecules in Dry Air

(Answers page 78.)

The warming of Earth's air by greenhouse gases is called the Greenhouse Effect. Without greenhouse gases the average temperature on Earth would be -18 °C (0 °F). At that temperature it would be so cold, the water on Earth, including that in the oceans, would freeze, and life as we know it would not exist. Greenhouse gases do not just keep the air warmer when it is daytime. They continue to radiate heat and warming Earth at night.

Energy from the sun passes through the walls of the greenhouse. Gas molecules inside the greenhouse absorb this energy and radiate it as heat, warming up the inside of the greenhouse. The walls of the greenhouse trap the heat inside, making the air warmer inside the greenhouse than it is outside. This warms greenhouses enough for plants to grow inside them during winter.

Not all of the sun's energy is absorbed; some of it is reflected back into space.

The temperature on Earth is a result of the amount of heat energy absorbed by molecules and the amount of heat that is reflected back into space. Something similar is happening in this house where the temperature inside is a result of the amount of heat entering it from the burning logs and the amount of heat exiting it through the front door.

Vibrating Molecules Heat Things Up
The Greenhouse Effect

Conducting an experiment where you observe the Greenhouse Effect is easier than you might think. All you need are some greenhouse gases, a device to monitor the temperature, energy from the sun, and a way to trap that energy. (Answers page 79 and 80.)

Materials

- 2 identical drinking glasses
- 2 Thermometers
- Tape
- Timer
- Vibrating Molecules Radiate Heat: The Greenhouse Effect Lab Sheet
- Plastic wrap
- Pen or pencil

Procedure

1. Tape the 2 thermometers, each to the inside of a different glass, 2 to 3 centimeters (cm) from the bottom of each glass. Make sure the tape does not cover the glass tube of the thermometer.
2. Carefully cover the top of one of the glasses with plastic wrap. The setup should be as air tight as possible. Tape the edges of the plastic wrap to the glass if you need to. Put both glasses in a sunny window or outside in the sun. Outside if the day is warm is best but not essential. The glass that is covered in plastic wrap is referred to as "enclosed space" and the glass that has no plastic wrap is referred to as "open space." This is in reference to the air being "enclosed" in the glass with the plastic wrap, and the air in the glass without the wrap being "open" to the air outside the glass.
3. Make a hypothesis about what you think will happen to the temperature in both glasses based on what you have learned. Write it on the lab sheet.
4. Wait one minute for the thermometers to stabilize and record the temperature of both thermometers for time = 0 on the lab sheet.
5. Record the temperatures of the thermometers every 5 minutes for 30 minutes.
6. Graph the data and answer the questions on the lab sheet.

Vibrating Molecules Heat Things Up
The Greenhouse Effect Lab Sheet

Hypothesis: How will the temperature vary in the enclosed space versus the open space?

Recording Data: Time 0 is when you begin recording data.

Time, minutes	Temperature, °C Enclosed Space	Temperature, °C Open Space
0		
5		
10		
15		
20		
25		
30		

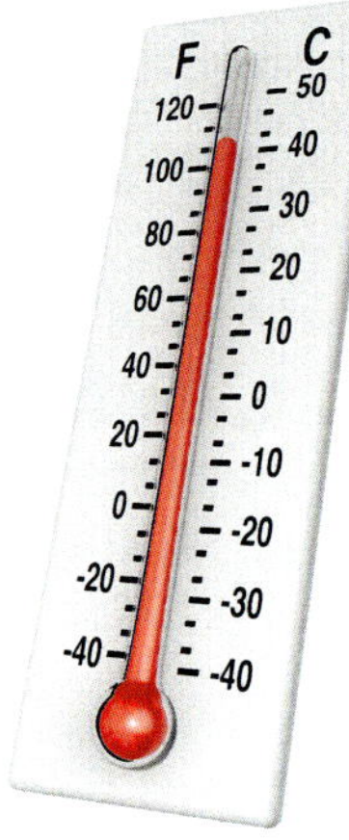

Use two different-colored pencils to record the temperature in the enclosed space and the open space. You will have two lines; one for the reading from each thermometer. Color in the legend on the right side to show which colored line goes with each temperature curve.

Temperature versus Time for the Air in an Enclosed Space and an Open Space

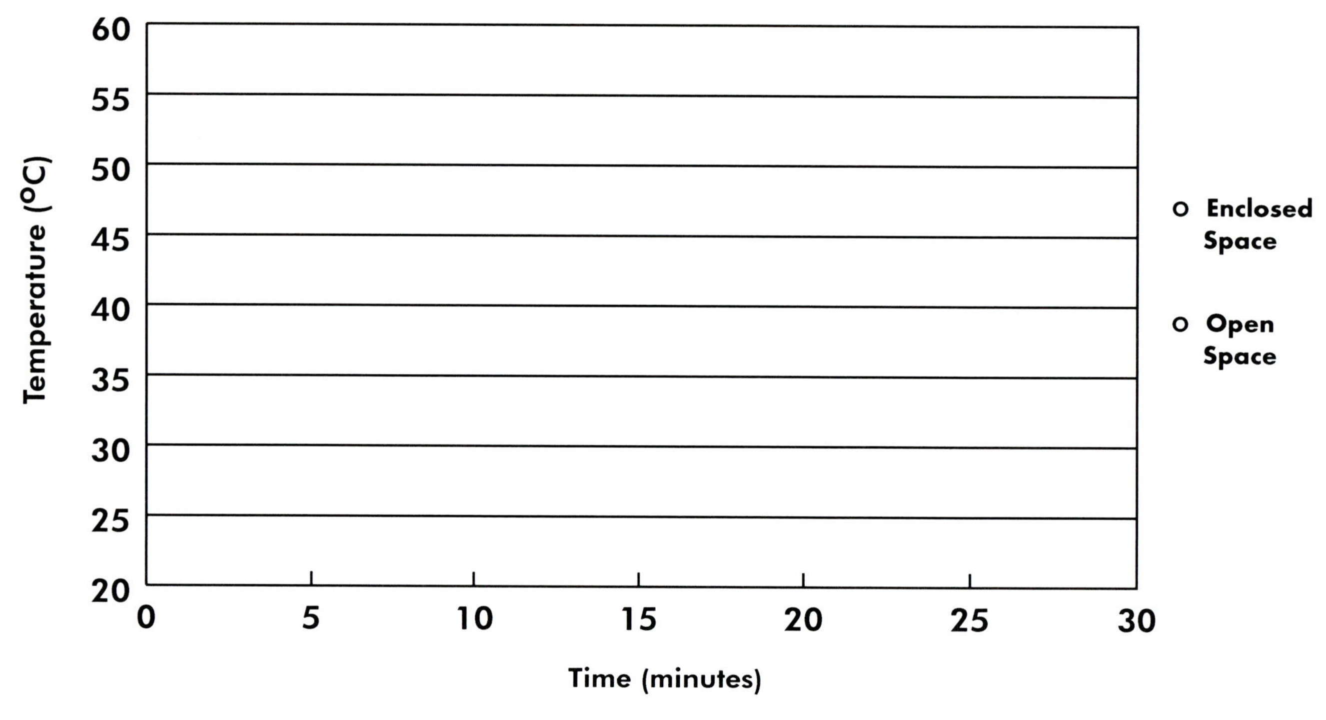

Questions for Vibrating Molecules Heat Things Up The Greenhouse Effect Lab Sheet

What is present in both glasses?

Were greenhouse gas molecules in both glasses? If yes, do you think the same concentration of greenhouse gas molecules is in both glasses?

What was the main difference between the two setups?

Describe what you observed for the temperature curves for the two setups, both the enclosed space and the open space.

Use what you have learned to explain what you observed.

Did your hypothesis do a good job of predicting what you observed? Why or why not?

If the amount of greenhouse gases increased in the glass that was enclosed what would you expect to happen? What if the amount decreased?

Earth isn't the only planet in the solar system that experiences a greenhouse effect. The planet Venus experiences what is sometimes called a "run-away" greenhouse effect. There are so many greenhouse gas molecules in Venus's air that the temperature reaches 462 °C (864 °F) at its surface.

PART 2: GLOBAL WARMING

Too Much of a Good Thing: Global Warming

Are you beginning to wonder when you are going to learn about climate change? Before you can understand climate change, you need to understand both the greenhouse effect and global warming.

A globe is a rounded spherical object. Earth is a globe, the moon is a globe, and some people have globes sitting on tables in their house. Scientists use the term global warming, because the warming happening now is happening everywhere across the globe, the spherical object that is Earth, and not just in local areas.

The story of global warming started over 200 years ago with the **Industrial Revolution**. The Industrial Revolution took place when animal and human power were replaced by machines. Machines were invented that produced electricity. Cars, planes, and trains are machines that allow people to travel much faster than riding a horse or walking. During the past 200 years people have come to rely on machines and the goods made by them. In fact, most of the things in your house were made by machines.

Even most homemade food starts with ingredients made by machines. Most fruits and vegetables are planted and harvested by machines.

Machine-Made or Not Activity

Look around your house to find things made by machines and those that were not. Then answer the questions below.

MACHINE-MADE	NOT MADE BY A MACHINE BUT TRANSPORTED OR HARVESTED BY A MACHINE	NOT MADE BY A MACHINE AND NOT TRANSPORTED BY A MACHINE

Which were easier to find, things made or transported by machines or things that were not?

Circle the items on your list that you could not have had before the Industrial Revolution, because they need electricity to run or to turn on.

What changes would have to be made to live without machines?

Have you noticed after you play hard that you get hungry? Is studying science making you crave something to eat? The food you eat and drink make the energy you need to work, including when that work is play. **Machines need energy to work, too**.

Machines get their energy from things you either wouldn't or couldn't eat.

Machines get energy from coal burning furnaces. Coal has hydrogen, carbon, oxygen, and nitrogen atoms in it.

Machines get energy from gasoline. Gasoline has hydrogen, carbon, oxygen, and nitrogen atoms in it.

Making Energy: The Combustion Reaction

Chemical reactions occur when the atoms in molecules combine, separate, or rearrange to make new and different molecules. Some chemical reactions release energy when these new molecules are made. **Machines get energy from a chemical reaction called the combustion reaction**.

The burning of wood is one example of the combustion reaction. Wood is made from molecules that contain carbon, oxygen, hydrogen, and nitrogen atoms. When wood burns in the presence of oxygen, the hydrogen, carbon, oxygen, and nitrogen molecules that made the molecules in wood rearrange and make the new molecules: carbon dioxide, methane, nitrous oxide, and water. There is also a large release of energy.

Most machines, including cars, get energy from materials, like coal, oil, and gasoline, which contain carbon, oxygen, nitrogen, and hydrogen. When these materials burn, they release the greenhouse gases—carbon dioxide, methane, and nitrous oxide—into the air.

Combustion Reactions Produce Energy

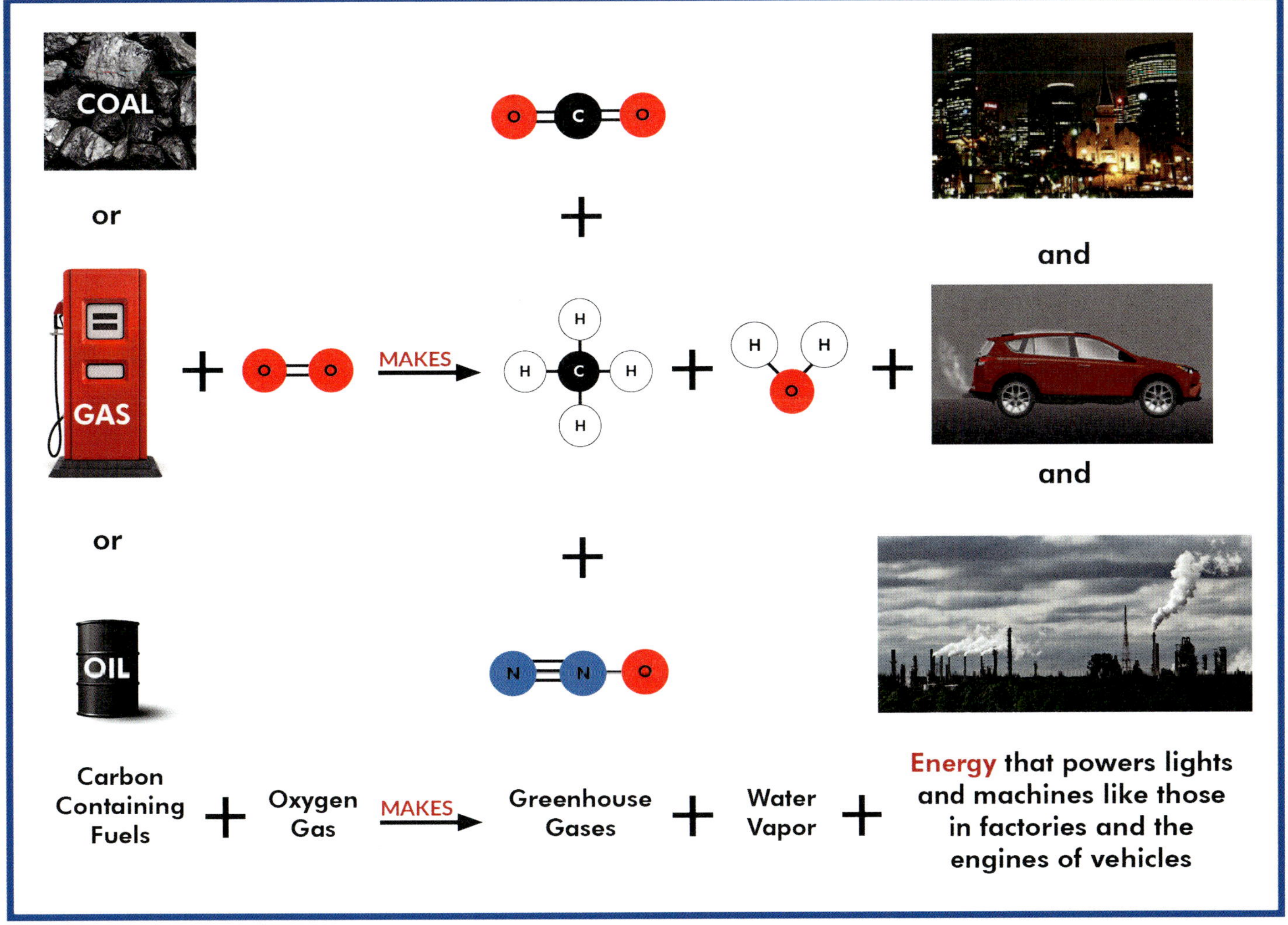

COAL or GAS or OIL + O=O MAKES O=C=O + CH_4 + N≡N–O + H–O–H + lights and car and factories

Carbon Containing Fuels + Oxygen Gas MAKES Greenhouse Gases + Water Vapor + **Energy** that powers lights and machines like those in factories and the engines of vehicles

In the Name of Science: An Activity Where You Generate Greenhouse Gases

You are about to be asked to do something in the name of science that you might not want to do, but you will learn from it. **You have already learned that gasoline, oil, coal, and wood, including wood products like paper, are made from molecules that have hydrogen, carbon, oxygen, and nitrogen in them, and that when they burn they make energy and the greenhouse gases: carbon dioxide, methane, nitrous oxide, and water. This is an important thing to understand.** Reading is a good way to learn, but not as good as actively participating in the process. This activity asks you to participate in the process of generating greenhouse gases. (Answers page 80.)

Materials

- A piece of paper
- A lighter or matches
- A car that is not an electric car
- A room with a light switch

Procedure

Over a sink or trash can have an adult light a piece of paper. Do you see the piece of paper disappearing as it burns? Some of the molecules that make the paper are carbon, hydrogen, and oxygen molecules. When the paper burns, those do not disappear into nothing. The paper molecules react with oxygen molecules in the air and make heat energy and the greenhouse gases: carbon dioxide and water vapor.

Ask an adult to open the hood of her car. Ask her to turn on the car. Now find the emission pipe of the car. Do not touch the emission pipe or the engine. Look at the engine. The engine is using gasoline to power it. When gasoline is used to make energy, it also makes the greenhouse gases: carbon dioxide, nitrous oxide, water vapor, and methane. Look at the exhaust pipe while the car is running. The greenhouse gases made during the combustion reaction that allows the car to run go into the air from the exhaust pipe. Next time you are driving, look at the vehicles on the road. All of them, with the exception of electric vehicles or fuel cell vehicles, have carbon dioxide, nitrous oxide, and methane coming from their exhaust pipes.

Turn on a light in your house. Where does the electricity come from that makes the light turn on? Electricity comes from power plants many miles or kilometers from your house. Most often, power plants use coal or natural gas to make electricity for people's houses. When coal or natural gas burn, they generate energy and the greenhouse gases: carbon dioxide, nitrous oxide, methane, and water vapor. The greenhouse gases are emitted from the smoke stacks at the power plants.

Choose one of the three scenarios above, and in words or drawings (or both) write the formula below for the combustion reaction that occurred when generating greenhouse gases.

Some of the greenhouse gases in the air are from natural sources. Natural sources of greenhouse gases are outgassing from volcanoes, forest fires, decomposing plant material, animal respiration, and cow farts. (Yes, those have greenhouse gases in them, and so do yours!)

Greenhouse gases are not "bad" molecules to have in the air. They moderate temperatures on Earth, which has been important for the evolution of life as we know it. It is the rapid increase in greenhouse gases since the Industrial Revolution that is the problem. It is too much of a good thing.

The smoke coming from the vent at the top of this volcano has greenhouse gases in it. The escape of gas is called outgassing. Volcanoes are a natural source of greenhouse gases.

Time for Some Math: How Many More?

(This activity refers to the box you made.)

Table 4: Get your calculator out and figure out how much the concentration of the three greenhouse gas molecules has increased. Subtract the number of molecules of each greenhouse gas that would have been in the air in the box **before** the Industrial Revolution from the number of molecules in there **now**. The number of molecules in column 2 will be subtracted from the number of molecules in column 1. Write the answer in column 3. (Answers page 80.)

COLUMN 1	COLUMN 2	COLUMN 3
December 2018 Your Box Would Have Contained	**Before the Industrial Era** Your Box Would Have Contained	**How Many More Are in Your Box?**
81,800,000,000,000,000 **carbon dioxide molecules**	56,000,000,000,000,000 **carbon dioxide molecules**	**carbon dioxide molecules**
372,600,000,000,000 **methane molecules**	158,000,000,000,000 **methane molecules**	**methane molecules**
66,400,000,000,000 **nitrous oxide molecules**	52,600,000,000,000 **nitrous oxide molecules**	**nitrous oxide molecules**

This is the increase in the number of these three greenhouse gas molecules in every 8 cubic centimeters of air all over Earth during the past 200 years. The concentration of greenhouse gases is increasing much faster at this time as more people buy and use more machine-made products, drive and fly more, and use more electricity. Today, your box has more greenhouse gas molecules in it than it would have contained in December 2018.

Think about how small your box is. WOW! That is a big increase in heat-trapping molecules in the air. The increase in the number of these greenhouse gas molecules is why the globe, Earth, is warming. Because of the Greenhouse Effect, the more greenhouse gases there are in the air, the hotter Earth is. The average surface temperature on Earth has risen over the past century. This increase in temperature is called **global warming**.

How Do Scientists Know the Concentration of Greenhouse Gases in the Air?

Scientists use **ice cores** to study Earth's climate as far back as 650,000 years before today. Scientists drill through ice sheets in Greenland and Antarctica and pull up core samples like the one this scientist is holding. **When the ice formed, the air from that time period was trapped in bubbles**. Scientists analyze the air bubbles to learn what the exact concentration of gases in the air was at that time. Graph 1 shows data scientists have recorded for the past 400,000 years.

Photo Credit NASA

The Concentration of Carbon Dioxide Gas for the Past 400,000 Years

CO_2 parts per million
440
420
400
380
360
340
320
300
280
260
240
220
200
180
160
* current CO_2 level
For 650,000 years, atmospheric CO_2 has never been above this line ... until now
1950
400,000 350,000 300,000 250,000 200,000 150,000 100,000 50,000 0
YEARS before today (0 = 1950)
* as of July 2013
GLOBAL CLIMATE CHANGE
climate.nasa.gov

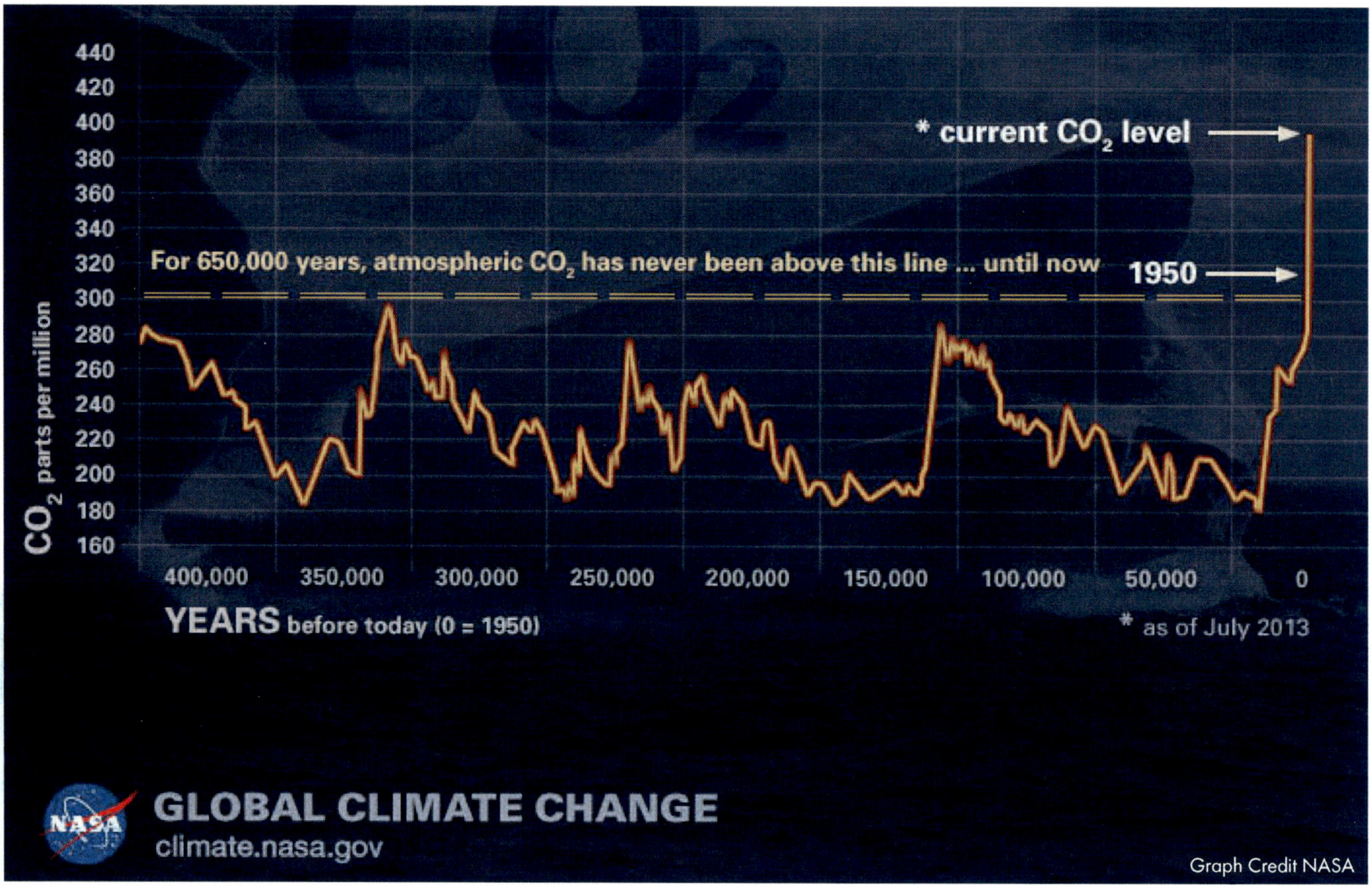

Graph Credit NASA

Graph 1: The concentration of the greenhouse gas, carbon dioxide, is higher now than it has been for over 400,000 years. As of 2020, the carbon dioxide concentration is over 412 ppm and rising.

Scientists use **infrared (IR) spectroscopy** to determine the presence and to measure the concentrations of greenhouse gases in air bubbles trapped 650,000 years ago and in the air collected at this time. As you have learned, some molecules vibrate in the presence of certain types of energy. Infrared radiation is one type of energy that causes greenhouse gas molecules to vibrate. Each type of molecule vibrates differently than any other type of molecule. How a molecule vibrates and the specific type of energy that makes it vibrate can be thought of as a molecule's "fingerprint."

All carbon dioxide molecules have the same "fingerprint," the same IR spectrum. All carbon dioxide molecules vibrate the same way when exposed to the same type of energy, this is different from how any other type of molecule vibrates. Every type of molecule has its own unique IR spectrum, including nitrous oxide, methane, and water vapor. When a sample of air is exposed to infrared radiation, each molecule present in the air vibrates in a specific way that only that type of molecule vibrates. Detectors measure the different types of vibrational signals and separates them out determining the types and quantities of each molecule present in the air. The detectors report the molecules present by producing IR spectrum, like those below, for each molecule detected.

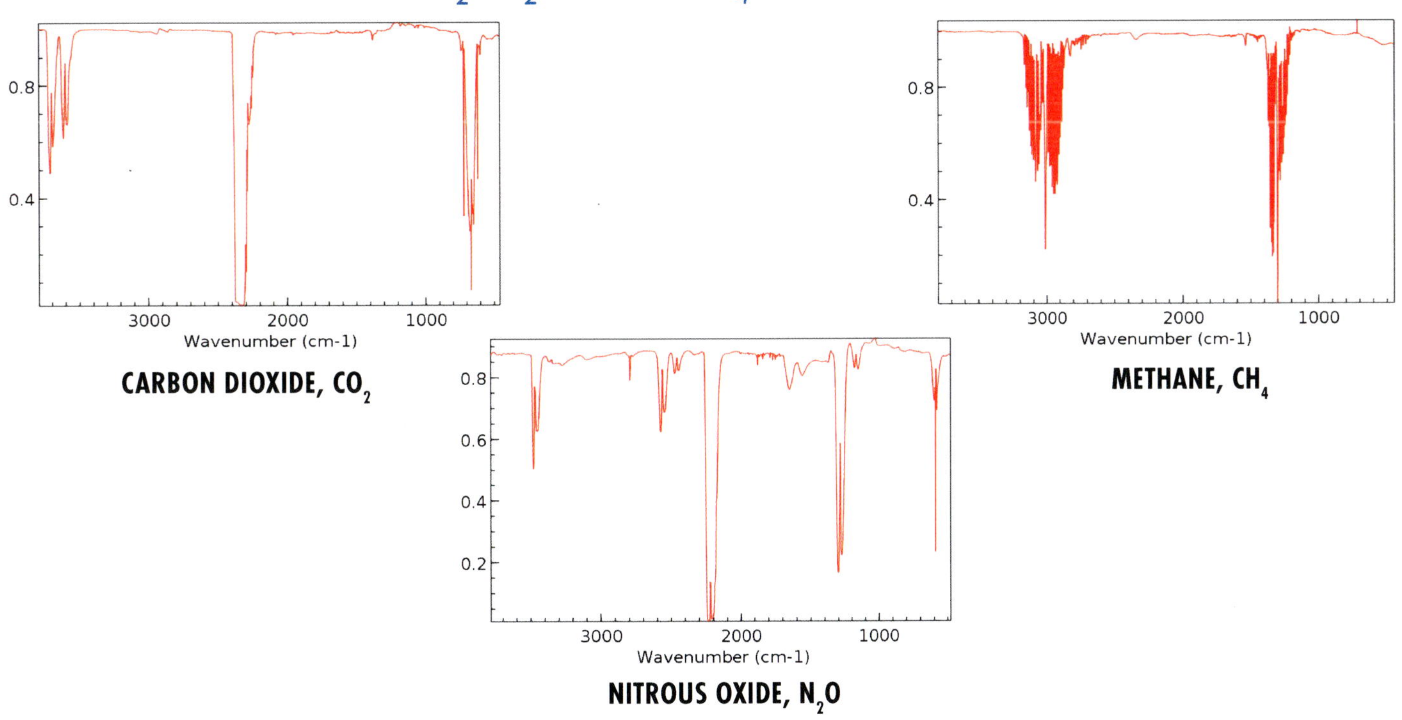

Graph the Concentrations of Greenhouse Gases

You can graph the increases in greenhouse gases just like scientists do. Graphs help to observe trends like the increase in greenhouse gases. For this activity, you will complete three graphs, graphing the data for the concentration of carbon dioxide, methane, and nitrous oxide. From the graphs you will be able to see how the concentrations are changing over time.

For this activity you will need a pen or pencil and the graph templates. There are two sets of graphs: Version A and Version B. Each set has three graphs in it. If you choose to do Version A, you will need the data table that is in Appendix 2, page 73. Version B contains dot-to-dot graphs. The second set of graphs uses the same data as the first set. **You only need to do one of the two versions**. Complete the questions after you have completed each graph. (Answers pages 81 and 82.)

Instructions

1. Use the concentration data from the Data Table in Appendix 2, page 73, to determine where to put the points on the graphs. The first data point is for the year 2000, which is on the y-axis. Graph all 19 points. When you have put all the points on the graph, connect the points starting at the y-axis going from left to right across the page.
2. Do this for the 3 graphs.
3. Each point shows the average concentration for that greenhouse gas during that year.
4. Based on the trend you observe for the 19-year period, hypothesize what you expect the average concentration of each greenhouse gas to be in 2020. Add a point to your graph for the year 2019 showing your prediction. Label it: "My Hypothesis."

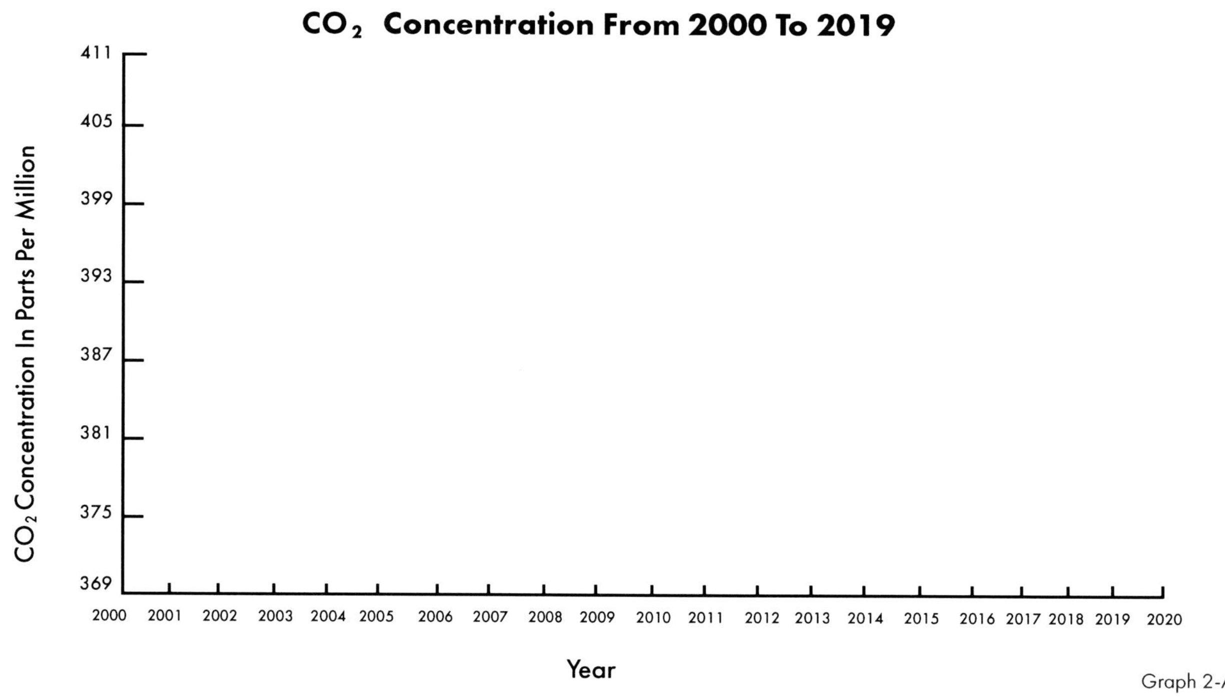

Graph 2-A

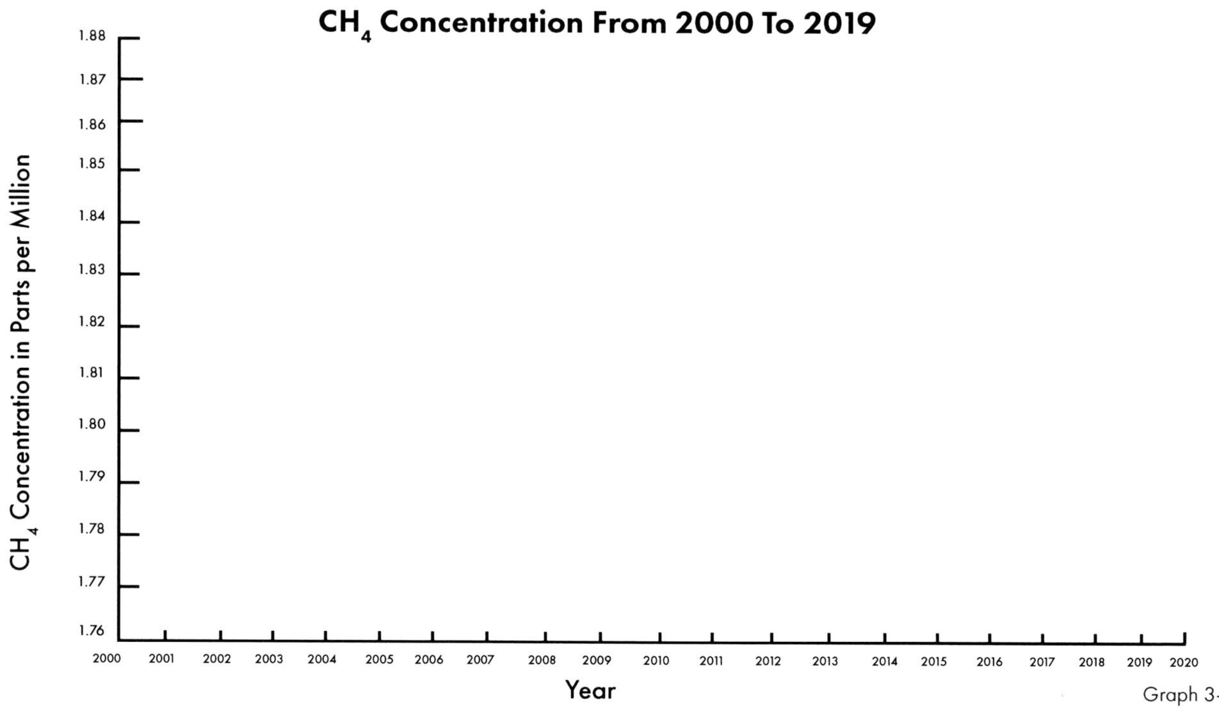

Graph 3-A

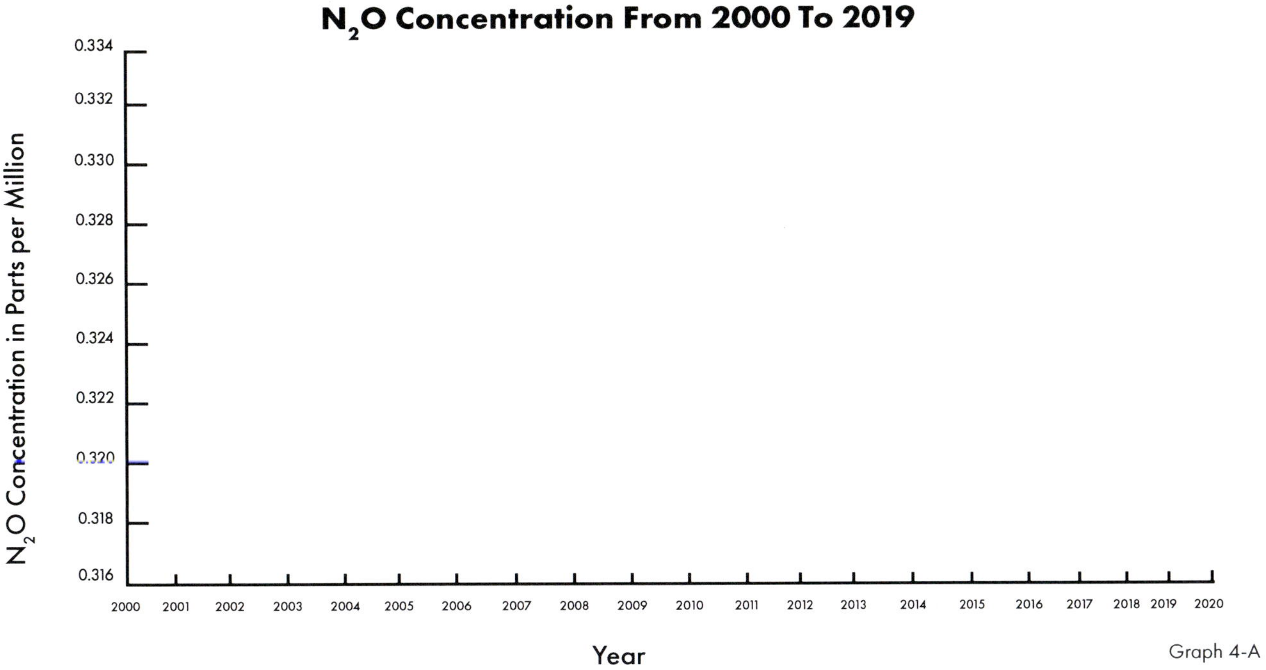

Graph 4-A

Questions

Do you wonder where the data for these graphs came from? If not, you should. Anytime you are given data, you should think like a scientist and ask what the source for the data is. This data was collected by scientists who work for The National Oceanic & Atmospheric Administration, NOAA, at the Earth Systems Laboratory in Mauna Loa, Hawaii: https://www.esrl.noaa.gov.

Now that you have worked with the data, it is time to make some conclusions based on the trends you observe on each graph.

Are the concentrations of the three greenhouse gases increasing or decreasing?

Do you think the concentration of these gases will increase of decrease over the next several years?

With the understanding that these gases trap the sun's energy and heat the air by radiating this energy as heat, do you conclude that the average global temperature will increase, decrease, or stay the same? Give an explanation for your conclusion.

Instructions

1. Start with the dot on the y-axis on the far right-hand side of the graph. Connect one dot at a time going from left to right across the page.
2. Do this for the 3 graphs.
3. Each point shows the average concentration for that greenhouse gas during that year.
4. Based on the trend you observe for the 1-year period, hypothesize what you expect the average concentration of each greenhouse gas to be in 2020. Add a point to your graph for the year 2020 showing your prediction. Label it: "My Hypothesis."

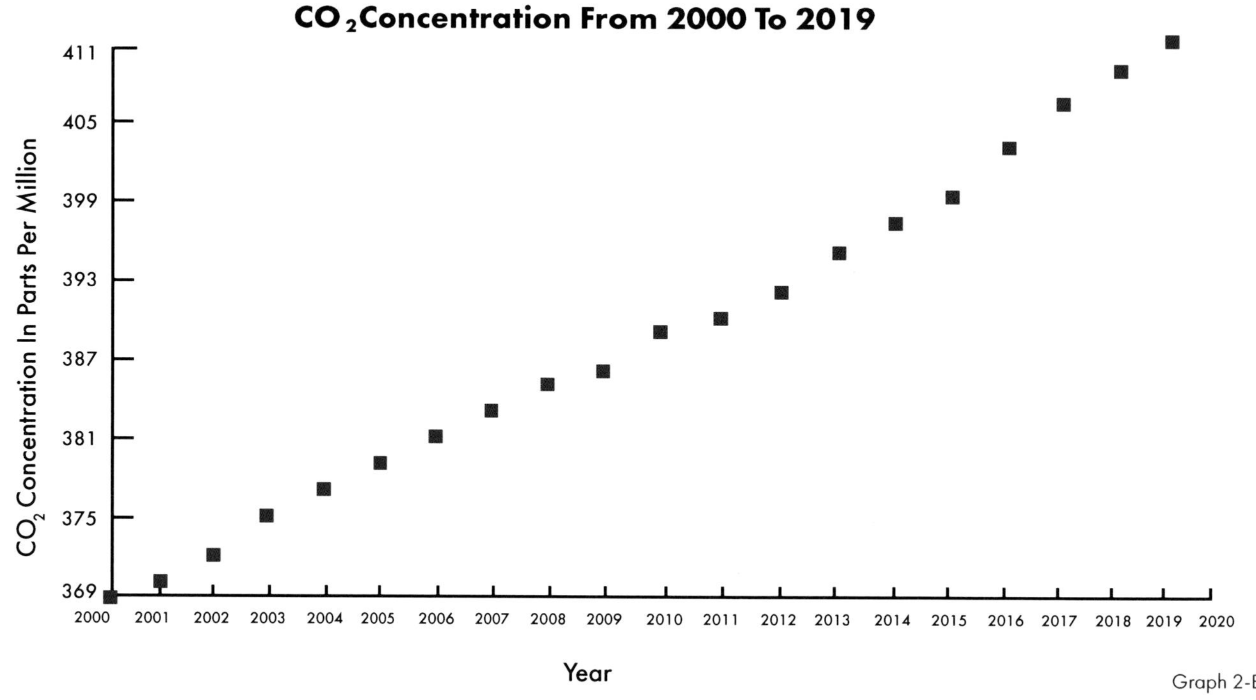

Graph 2-B

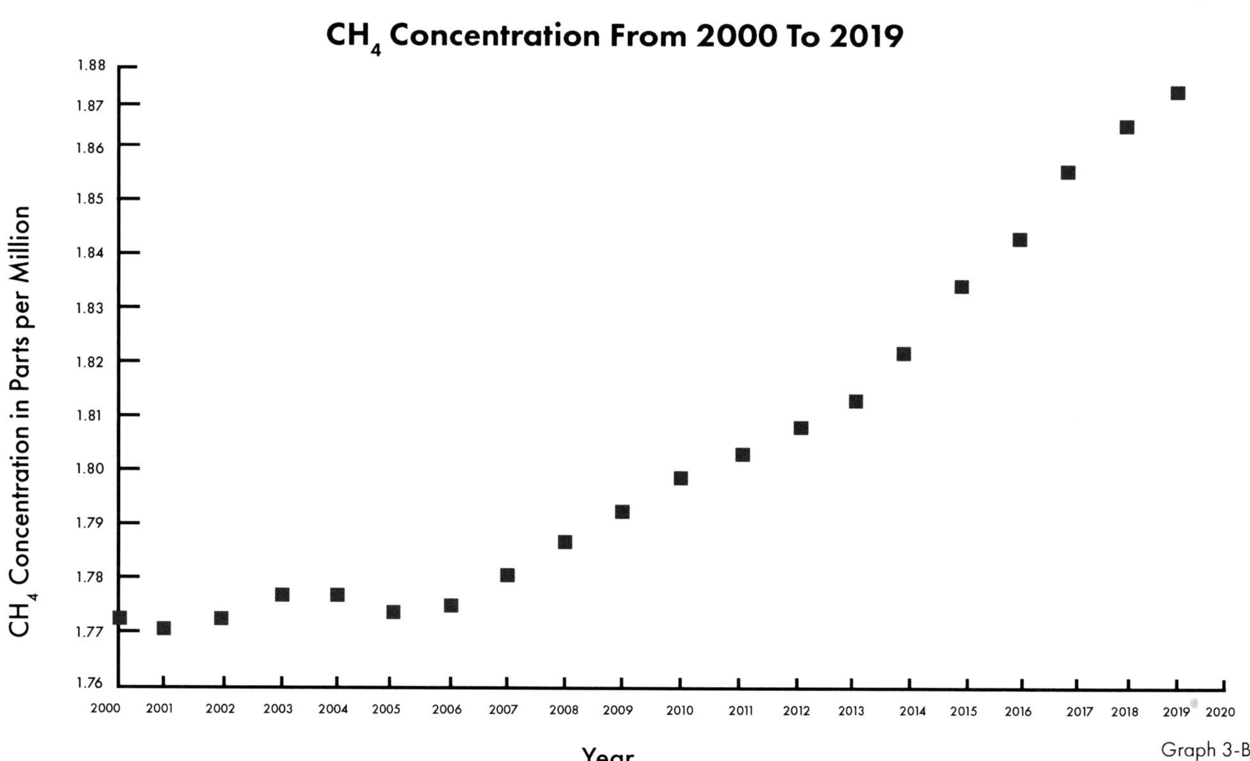

Graph 3-B

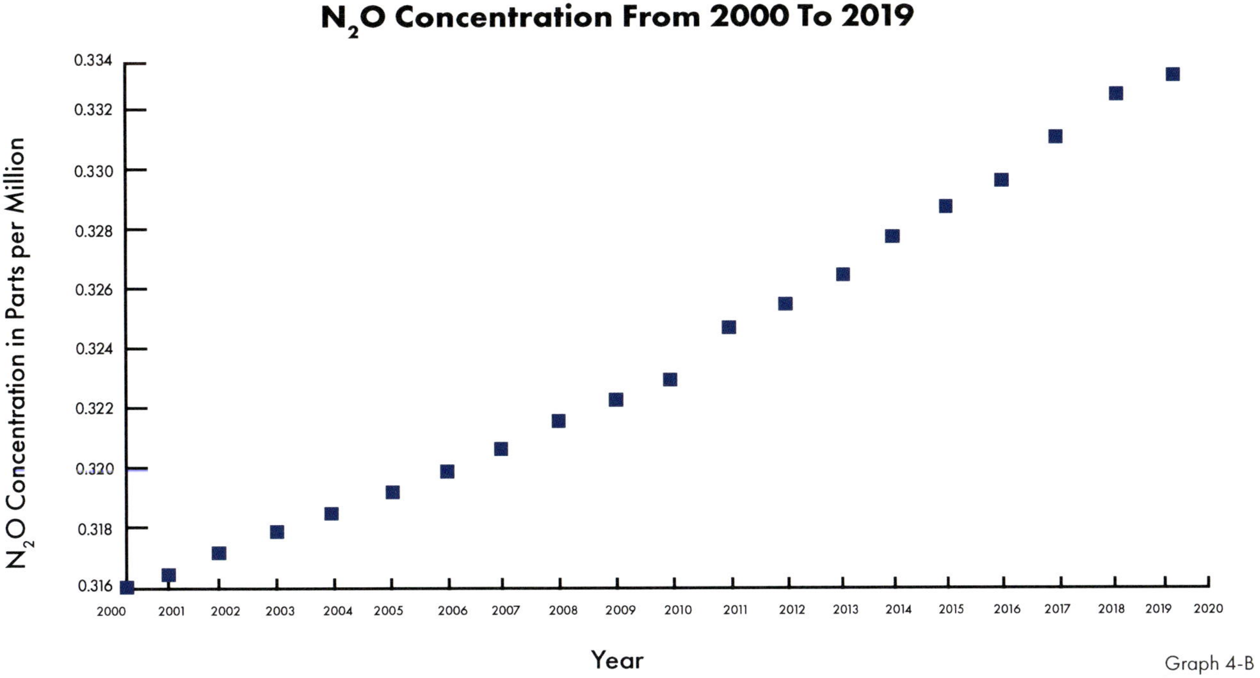

Graph 4-B

Questions

Do you wonder where the data for these graphs came from? If not, you should. Anytime you are given data, you should think like a scientist and ask what the source for the data is. This data was collected by scientists who work for The National Oceanic & Atmospheric Administration, NOAA, at the Earth Systems Laboratory in Mauna Loa, Hawaii: https://www.esrl.noaa.gov.

Now that you have worked with the data, it is time to make some conclusions based on the trends you observe on each graph.

Are the concentrations of the three greenhouse gases increasing or decreasing?

Do you think the concentration of these gases will increase of decrease over the next several years?

With the understanding that these gases trap the sun's energy and heat the air by radiating energy as heat, do you conclude that the average global temperature will increase, decrease, or stay the same? Give an explanation for your conclusion.

Putting extra blankets over you when you are cold helps keep you warmer, because **blankets absorb and trap your body heat**. The more body heat that is trapped, the warmer you are.

Increasing the number of heat-trapping molecules is similar to increasing the number of blankets. **As the concentration of greenhouse gas molecules increases, more heat energy is absorbed, "trapped," and radiated, which warms the air.**

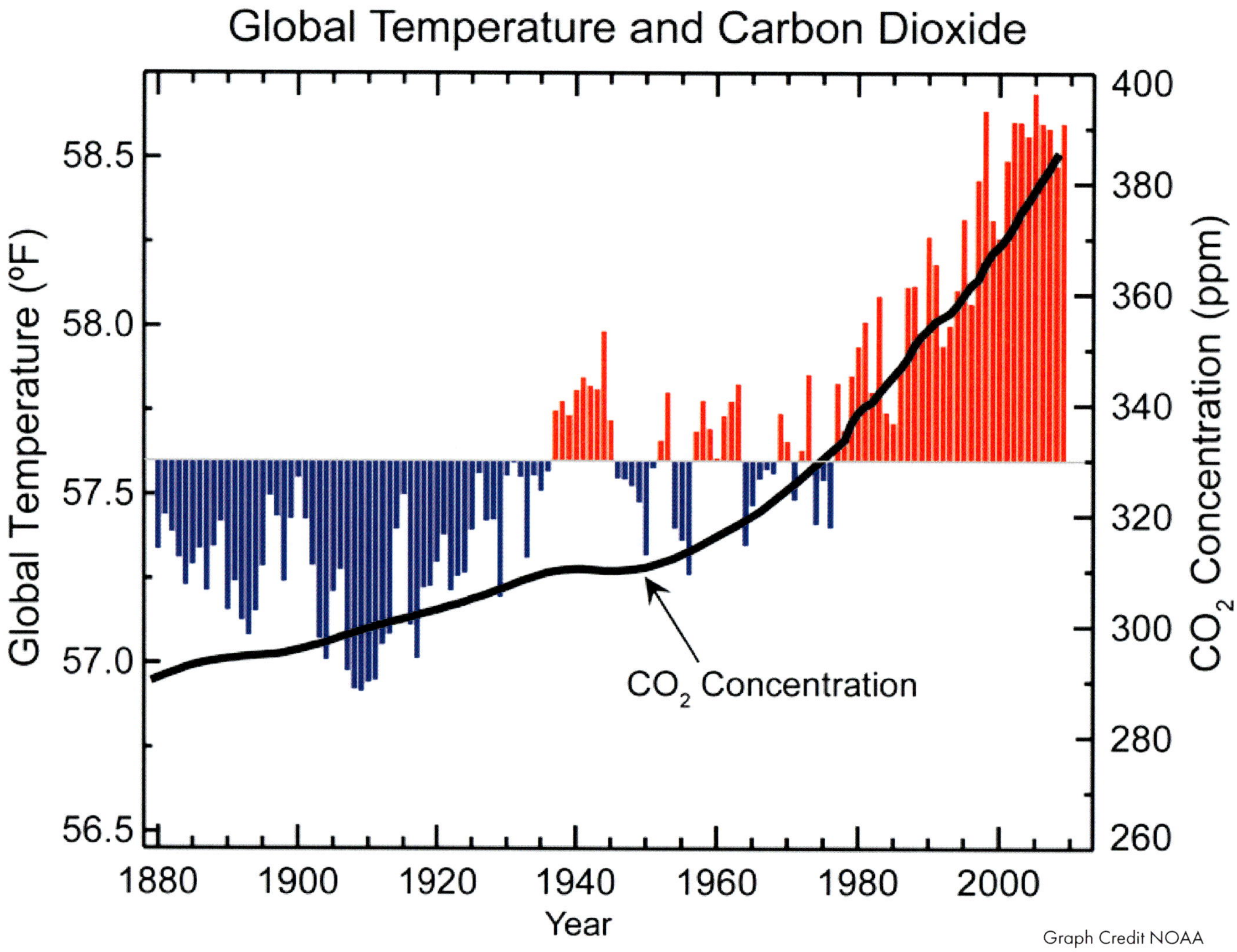

Global Temperature and Carbon Dioxide

Global Temperature (°F): 56.5, 57.0, 57.5, 58.0, 58.5

CO_2 Concentration (ppm): 260, 280, 300, 320, 340, 360, 380, 400

Year: 1880, 1900, 1920, 1940, 1960, 1980, 2000

CO_2 Concentration

Graph Credit NOAA

Graph 5: This graph, spanning from 1880 to 2009, shows the increase in the global temperature as the concentration of carbon dioxide has increased in the air since the Industrial Revolution. This increase in temperature is called global warming.

Between the time of the Industrial Revolution and now, the average global temperature increased 0.94°C (1.69°F). The five hottest years on record are 2014, 2015, 2016, 2017, and 2018. 2019 is expected to be even hotter.

0.94°C (1.69°F) does not seem like much of a temperature increase, does it?

Think about this for a moment though. Think about how much energy it takes to heat the air inside your house when it is cold. Now think about how much more of the sun's energy molecules in the air must be transferring, absorbing and radiating, to heat something the size of Earth!

The World's Oceans Have Warmed, Too

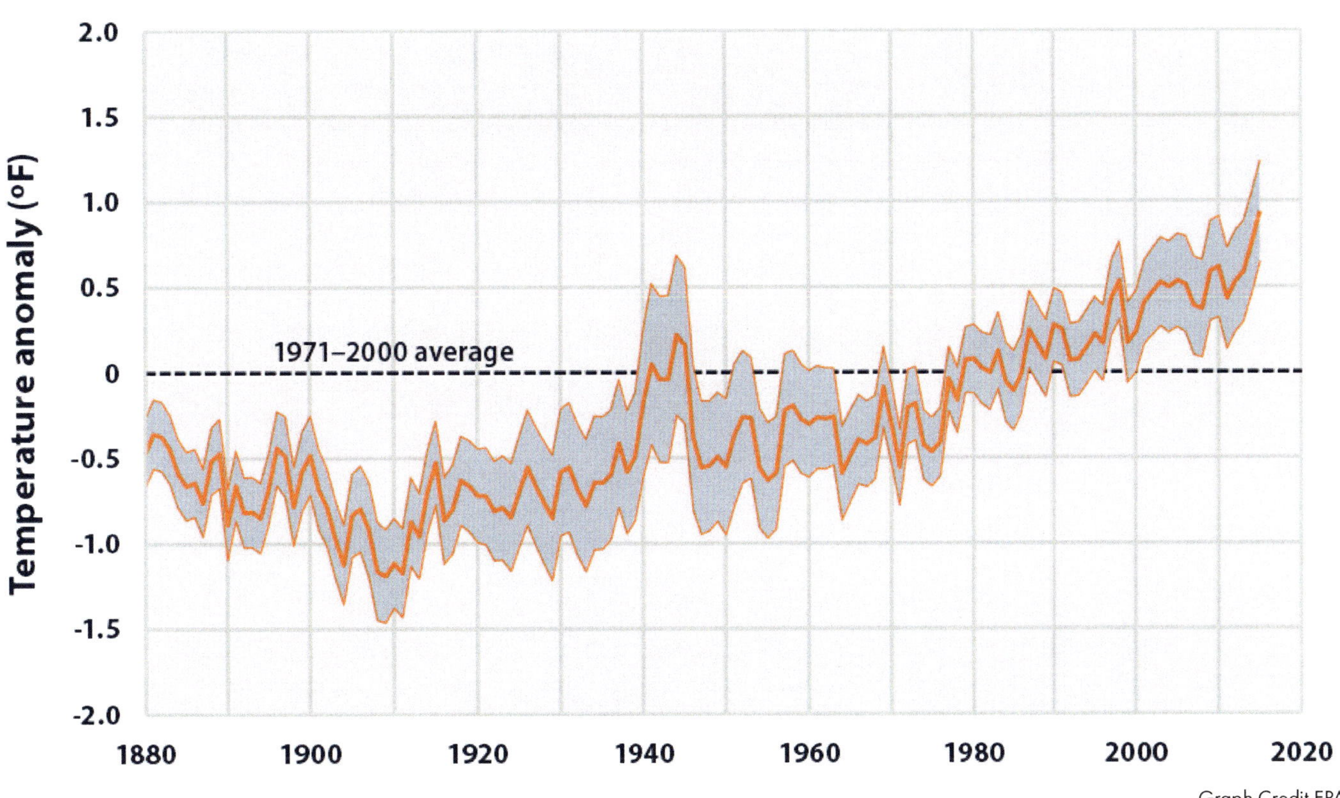

Graph 6: There has been a steady increase in the average surface temperature for the world's oceans as shown on this graph.

Warmer Air Leads to Warmer Waters

When the air warms for an extended period of time, as is happening now, so does the water in the oceans. The National Oceanic and Atmospheric Association, NOAA, estimates that there are 1,338,000,000.09 cubic kilometers (321,003,271 cubic miles) of water in the ocean. That is a lot of water to heat up! Probably because people live on land, the focus is on the temperature increase that is happening in the air. Seventy-one percent of Earth's surface is covered by ocean. It is estimated that more than 90 percent of the warming over the past 50 years has happened in the ocean. Global warming is happening to the entire surface of the globe.

2012-2016
2
1
0
-1
-2
°C
Map Credit NASA
The world's oceans have also warmed. Many fish, coral, and aquatic plants do not like it when water warms.
Average temperatures of the North and South Poles have increased the most, melting ice, snow, and glaciers at record rates. The closer to the equator you get, the smaller the amount the average temperature has increased.

Feedback Mechanisms

A **feedback mechanism** is a loop system, where the occurrence of one thing leads to something else, which through one or more events causes the system to respond in the same direction (**a positive feedback loop**) or the opposite direction (**a negative feedback loop**). The warming of Earth's land and water is triggering natural events that are causing several positive feedback loops that are increasing the **rate** of warming, and in some cases the number of greenhouse gases in the air.

Water molecules in the gas state are called water vapor.

Air has water molecules in it. If you have ever watched a pot of water boiling on the stove, you know that when water heats, water vapor rises out of the water and becomes part of the air. There doesn't need to be boiling water to have water vapor in the air. If the air temperature over a body of water increases by even a small amount, there will be more water vapor at that location. <u>Water vapor is an important greenhouse gas</u>.

26 °C (79 °F)

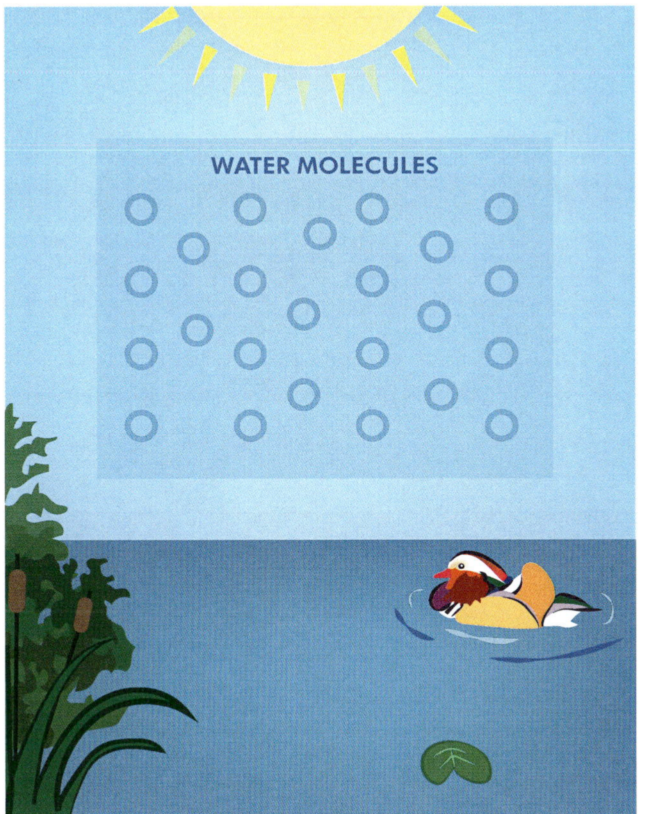

24 °C (75 °F)

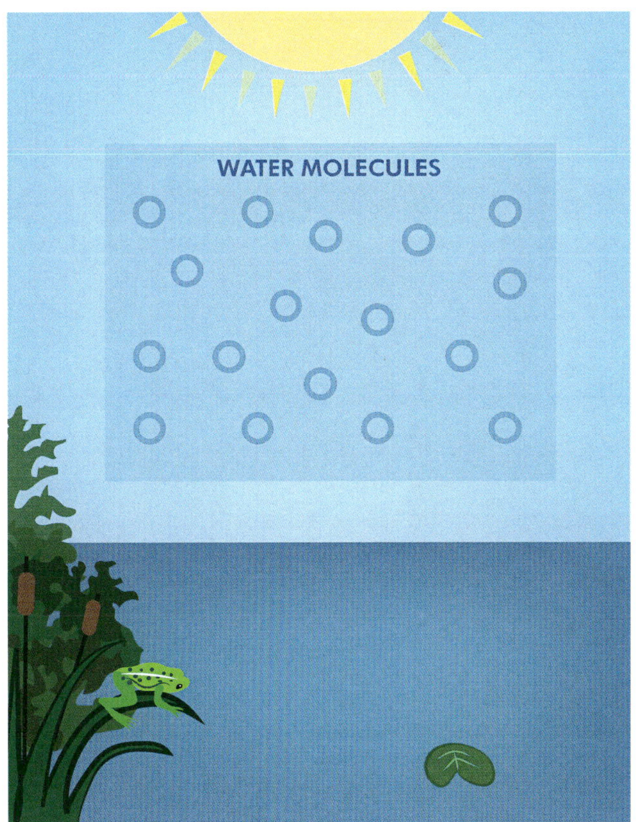

There are more water vapor molecules in the column where the air is 26 °C.

The warmer the air is, the more water vapor there is in the air. The more water vapor there is in the air, the more of the sun's energy water molecules absorb. The more of the sun's energy water vapor absorbs, the more heat the molecules radiate. The more heat the molecules radiate, the warmer the air is. It is a cycle. **This type of cycle is called a positive feedback loop**.

The average global air temperature increases.

Warmer air and melting sea ice warm the world's oceans.

Warmer ocean waters result in more water vapor molecules in the air.

Water vapor is a greenhouse gas. More water vapor in the air means more of the sun's energy is trapped and radiated as heat.

Positive feedback loops, like this one, increase the rate of global warming.

Graph Credit NOAA

Higher Temperatures Cause Ice Sheets and Glaciers to Melt.

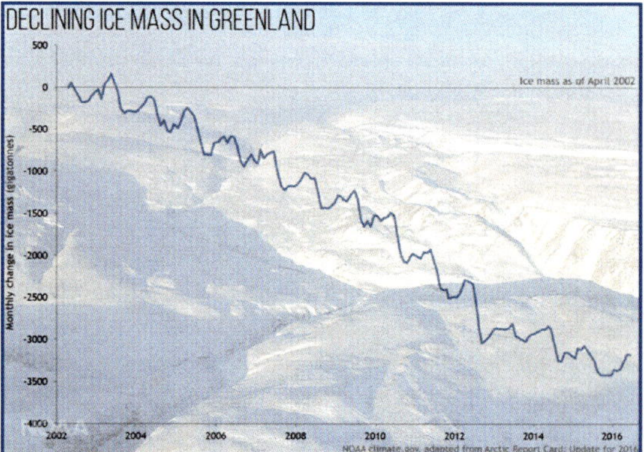

Graph Credit NOAA

Ice has a high albedo. Albedo is a measure of reflectivity. Things with high albedo reflect more of the sun's energy. Lower albedo means less of the sun's energy is reflected back into space.

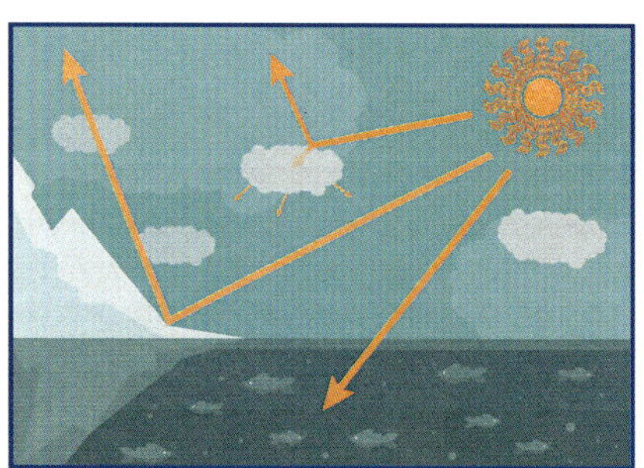

The permafrost above was covered with ice and snow. When ice melts, the albedo lowers. Water and the newly exposed land absorb the sun's energy instead of reflecting it.

The Global Temperature Increases.

This is a Positive Feedback Loop

Each event feeds into the next event creating a loop system continuously responding in the same direction.

Make a Positive Feedback Loop for Methane

There is a second positive feedback loop involving permafrost. Permafrost is a layer of permanently frozen soil that extends 25 to 100 cm deep. Methane is trapped beneath the permafrost. When the permafrost melts, methane gas is released into the atmosphere. The released methane molecules absorb energy, and then radiate the energy as heat, which in turn melts more of the snow and ice covering the permafrost. The higher temperatures melt the newly exposed permafrost, and the cycle begins again.

First watch this video showing methane bubbling from the surface, https://climate.nasa.gov/news/2785/unexpected-future-boost-of-methane-possible-from-arctic-permafrost/. Then use illustrations, photos, words, or a combination of all three to create a positive feedback loop for this cycle. The first step has been done for you. (Answer page 83.)

The Temperature Increases.

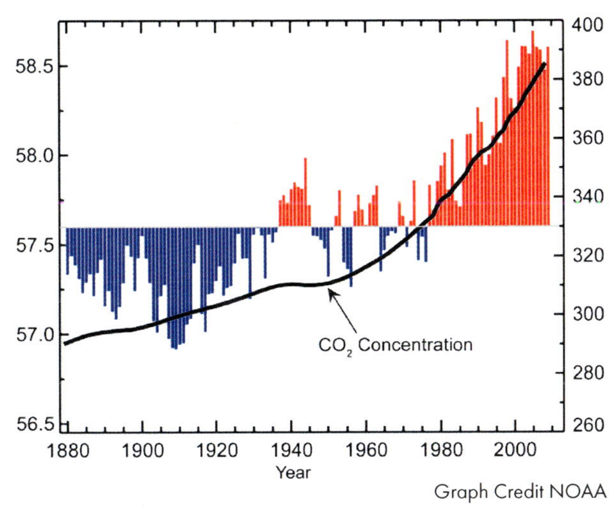

Graph Credit NOAA

The Increase in Greenhouse Gases Is Causing Global Warming
The more heat-trapping molecules there are in the air, the more heat that gets absorbed.
ENERGY
AIR
EARTH
CH_4 N_2O H_2O CO_2
The same amount of energy from the sun travels to Earth. There has been an increase in greenhouse gas molecules since the Industrial Revolution. The more heat that gets transferred to the air, the warmer the weather is.
The rise in temperature is an average for the entire globe. The rise of the temperature in some places, like the North and South Poles, is more than **0.94°C**.

PART 3: CLIMATE CHANGE

First a Word about the Weather

When scientists talk about climate change, they are talking about long-term changes in the weather. Climate and weather both describe the temperature, **precipitation** (rain and snowfall), and wind in an area. **The difference between weather and climate has to do with the amount of time each is measured.** **Weather** is a short-term measurement, measured in hours and days. **Climate** is a long-term measurement, measured using weather data averages collected over 30 or more years.

Weather is the temperature, precipitation, and wind happening today, tomorrow, or a week from now. You might even talk about the weather last year. When you talk about the typical weather during a season of the year, however, you are referring to the climate. That is because the "typical weather" in an area is determined by averaging weather data collected over many years. It is a long-term measurement.

What is happening today is the weather.

The Weather

Fill in the Table below with information about yesterday's weather where you live.

What was the weather outside your house yesterday?

Location:

Date:

Temperature:

Rain, Snow, or Sunshine:

Windy or Calm:

Look back at Graph 5, page 34. Each year the average global temperature varies from the year before and the year to come. That is why scientists use a long-term average to determine if and when the climate is changing.

To determine the climate of an area, scientists examine the weather for 30 or more years. This information gives scientists a good idea about what type of weather can be expected during specific times of the year and for certain weather conditions. **Meteorologists**, people who study and make predictions about the weather, use data collected over many years to predict the weather.

The **weather** that happened on this date every year for the past 30 years or more when averaged together tells what the **climate** is.

OCTOBER 15, 2017
WARM AND SUNNY

2016 WARM AND CLOUDY	2006 COOL AND RAINY	1996 COLD AND SUNNY
2015 WARM AND RAINY	2005 WARM AND CLOUDY	1995 COOL AND SUNNY
2014 WARM AND SUNNY	2004 COLD AND RAINY	1994 WARM AND CLOUDY
2013 COOL AND SUNNY	2003 COLD AND CLOUDY	1993 COOL AND SUNNY
2012 WARM AND RAINY	2002 COOL AND SUNNY	1992 COLD AND RAINY
2011 COOL AND CLOUDY	2001 WARM AND RAINY	1991 WARM AND SUNNY
2010 WARM AND CLOUDY	2000 COOL AND SUNNY	1990 COLD AND CLOUDY
2009 WARM AND RAINY	1999 COLD AND CLOUDY	1989 COLD AND SUNNY
2008 COOL AND SUNNY	1998 WARM AND RAINY	1988 COLD AND CLOUDY
2007 COOL AND RAINY	1997 COOL AND SUNNY	1987 COOL AND SUNNY

You have recorded the weather at your house. To determine what the climate is for yesterday's date at your house, you need to collect the weather data for 30 years. After that, you need to do some math to calculate the averages.

The Climate: What has the Weather Been at My House for the Past 30 Years?

In this activity, you will look up what the average temperature, total amount of precipitation, and the average wind speed have been in your neighborhood every year for the past 30 years. You will use this data to determine the climate where you live for yesterday's date. (Answers pages 83 to 85.)

Materials

- A pen or pencil
- Internet access
- The Data Table for What Has the Weather Been at My House for the Past 30 Years
- Calculator *Optional: You might need help recording the data and calculating the 30-year averages.*

Procedure

1. Go to the link Weather Underground History, https://www.wunderground.com/history.
2. For "Location" enter your location.
3. For "Date" choose yesterday's date. The reason for using yesterday's date instead of today's date is that the weather for today is a prediction and yesterday's date is actual recorded data.
4. Click on the blue "Submit" button.
5. On the Data Table, in the second row, write the month and date but not the year. For example, March 11.
6. In the far left-hand column of the Data Table, write the year starting with the year it is, counting backwards for 30 years, ex. 2020, 2019, 2018...
7. Check the units on the Weather Underground site before recording data. If your units are in °F and inches, go to the upper-right portion of the web page and click on the round gear-shaped symbol. Click on °C and the data will be reported using the metric system. (You can use °F, inches, and miles instead. If you do, remember to change your units at the top of each column of the Data Table.)
8. Write the temperature that is at the top of the left column under the heading "Temperature." This is the number for the "Actual Mean Temperature."
9. For the precipitation value you need to add the two values for precipitation and snow that are found under the headings "Precipitation" and "Snow." Both values are at the top of the left columns under these two headings.
10. Write the wind speed without its direction. This is at the top of the left column under the heading "Wind Speed."
11. Now that you have collected the raw data, it is time to calculate the climate measurements. The math is optional. If you don't do the math problems, look at the questions after each calculation. It is more important that you think through the data you have collected than to do the calculations for the specific numbers. If you need to, you can use the data and calculations from the answer key in Appendix 4, pages 85 to 87, to answer the questions.

What Has the Weather Been at My House for the Past 30 Years? Data Sheet

Data Table: The Climate: What has the weather been at My House for the past 30 years?

Write the Month and Date here but not the year:

YEAR	ACTUAL MEAN TEMPERATURE, °C	PRECIPITATION, CM	WIND SPEED, KPH

Calculate the 30-year averages for yesterday's date where you live.

Temperature: Use your calculator to add together the 30 temperature measurements you recorded. Write this number down before the sign for division. Use your calculator to divide this number by 30. Write the answer down after the equal sign. The answer is a 30-year average. It is the climate measurement for the temperature for yesterday's date where you live.

÷30 =

Precipitation: Use your calculator to add together the 30 precipitation measurements you recorded. Write this number down before the sign for division. Use your calculator to divide this number by 30. Write the answer down after the equal sign. The answer is a 30-year average. It is the climate measurement for the precipitation for yesterday's date where you live.

÷30 =

Wind Speed: Use your calculator to add together the 30 wind speed measurements you recorded. Write this number down before the sign for division. Use your calculator to divide this number by 30. Write the answer down after the equal sign. The answer is a 30-year average. It is the climate measurement for the wind speed for yesterday's date where you live.

÷30 =

Fill in the Table below to compare the climate measurements with the 1-day measurements, the weather measurement, from yesterday's date. Use the data for yesterday from the Data Table.

MEASUREMENTS	1-DAY WEATHER MEASUREMENT	30-YEAR CLIMATE MEASUREMENTS
Temperature		
Precipitation		
Wind Speed		

Use words to describe how the 1-day measurements compare with the 30-year averages. Use the data you collected and averages calculated in your answers.

Use the data in the Data Table to fill in the table below.

MEASUREMENTS	HIGHEST MEAN VALUE	LOWEST MEAN VALUE	RANGE*
Temperature			
Precipitation			
Wind Speed			

* Subtract the lowest value from the highest value to calculate the range.

To predict the weather for yesterday's date a year from now, would you use the climate measurements or the weather measurements? Give a reason for you choice.

The Evidence for Climate Change

Scientists used the scientific method to determine that climate change is happening. The **scientific method** uses logic to ask and answer questions about how the natural and physical world works. Scientists conduct experiments and examine the research of other scientists when developing a hypothesis. Once they have made a prediction about what is going on with the system, scientists conduct more experiments and draw one or more conclusions based on their data and observations. That is not the end of the process though. Before sharing the conclusions with the public, Scientists have their work evaluated by other scientists working in the same field. If the majority agree with the conclusions, then and only then, are the conclusions shared. This is the process that has been used to determine that rapid climate change is happening now, and that humans are responsible for it.

Image Credit Stacy Hargrove, NOAA

Scientists used the scientific method to determine that rising sea levels, caused by global warming, are swamping areas where endangered sea turtles make their nests.

The Scientific Method Has Six Steps

Step 1. Scientists make observations that lead then to ask a science question.

Step 2. Make observations focused on answering the question. An **observation** means to study carefully.

Step 3. Form a hypothesis. A **hypothesis** is a prediction based on observations.

Step 4. Design an experiment to test the hypothesis.

Step 5. Analyze the data from experiments and observations.

Step 6. Draw a Conclusion.

Scientists observed an increase in greenhouse gases in the air. They began to ask questions about how this was affecting Earth and life on it. Knowing the relationship between greenhouse gases, air temperature, weather, and climate, scientists formed a hypothesis that the increase in greenhouse gases was causing **global climate change.**

To learn if this hypothesis was correct, scientists designed experiments and analyzed data. Based on data and observations, scientists concluded that global warming is giving rise to global climate change and the cause is greenhouse gases generated by the endeavors of people.

Data and Observations

Data shows that the concentration of greenhouse gases in the air has increased because of the burning of coal, gasoline, and oil as people have come to rely more on machines and machine-made materials. The data show that the average global temperature rose 0.94°C (1.69°F) from 1880 to 2015. This data combined with observations from experiments shows that the increase in greenhouse gases is responsible for the increase in temperature.

In addition to the increase in the average global temperature, researchers have observed other changes occurring to the climate because of global warming.

Scientists have observed the occurrence of more powerful storms. The three key measurements for weather are temperature, precipitation, and wind speed. An increase in the global temperature of the air and ocean water affects global precipitation patterns and wind speed.

As ocean temperatures rise there is more water vapor in the **atmosphere**, air surrounding the planets. An increase in water vapor in the **atmosphere** causes changes in the amount of precipitation. Wind is air that is moving. The temperature of the ocean and air has a direct effect on wind patterns and wind speeds. Increases in ocean water temperatures, atmospheric (air) temperatures, and the concentration of water vapor in the air contribute to an increase in the intensity of hurricanes.

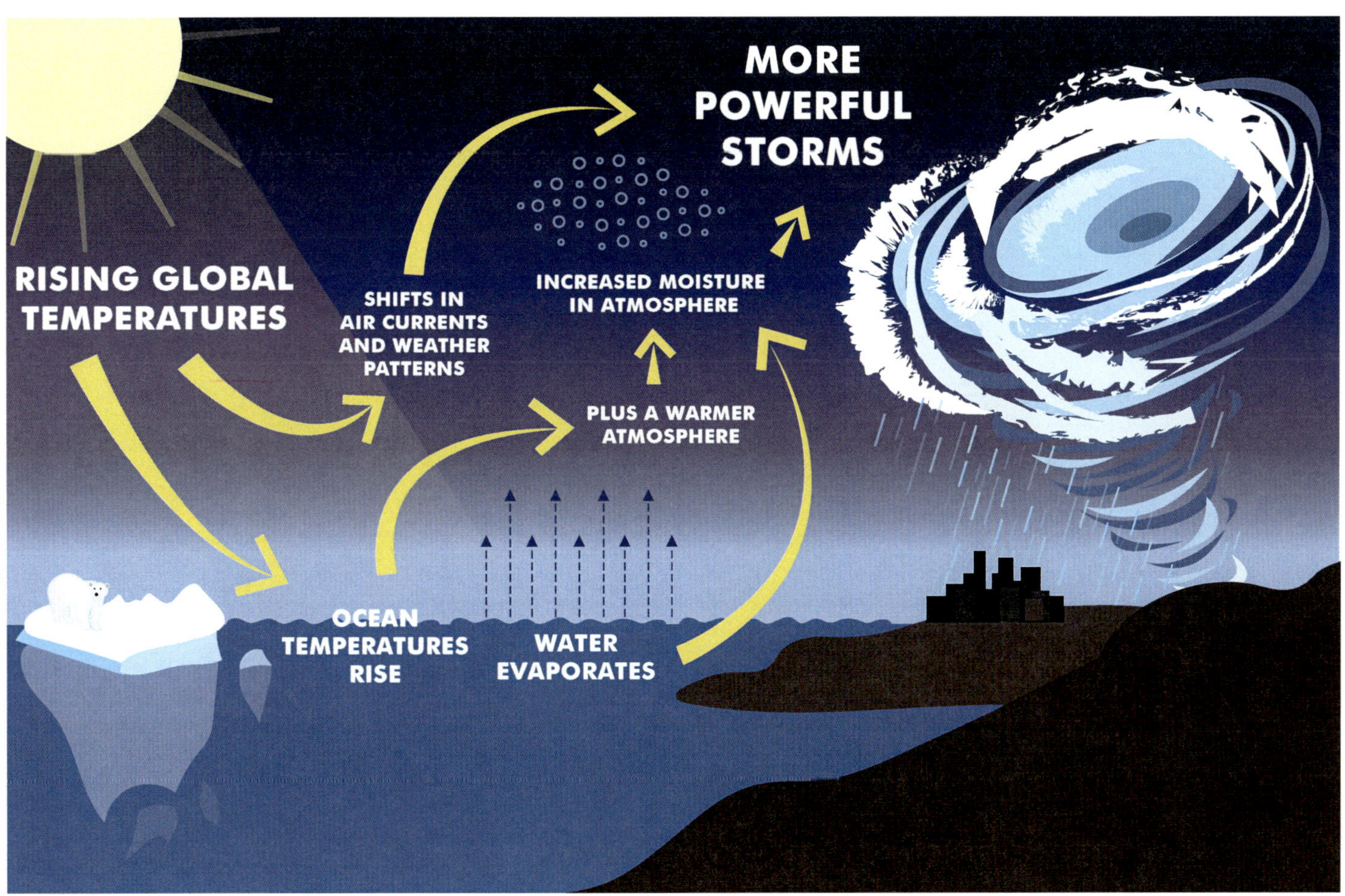

There has been more extreme weather such as droughts, increased wind speeds, and hurricanes during the past 30 years.

Rising Sea Level and Melting Ice Sheets

Photo Credit NOAA

This photograph shows the melting of an ice sheet in Greenland. The global sea level rose 17 cm (6.7 inches) during the past century. This happened in part because glaciers and Arctic ice melted into the sea. It's similar to how your bathtub would fill with liquid water if you put ice cubes in it and let them melt.

The sea level is also rising because of the increase in the temperature of the ocean's water. When water heats, as is happening in the world's oceans, it expands. The expansion of water at a higher temperature is shown in the illustration below.

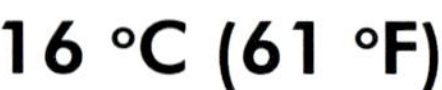

16 °C (61 °F)

18 °C (64.5 °F)

The increase in volume with increased temperature is called **thermal expansion.**

The chemistry of ocean water is also changing, in a process called ocean acidification. **Ocean acidification** is just what it sounds like; ocean waters are becoming more acidic. Ocean acidification is damaging to coral reefs. It is also causing the shells of marine animals such as sea snails to dissolve.

Day 0

Day 15

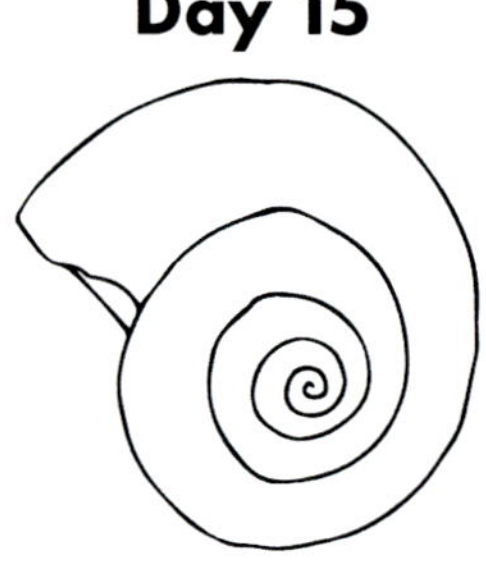

Day 30

Day 45

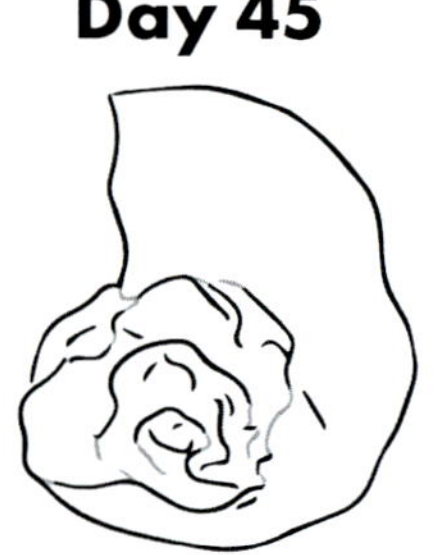

Illustration Credit Pandia Press

Scientists predict the oceans will become more acidic. This small sea snail was put in ocean water with the acidity expected by 2100. The solution to stopping the increased acidification of ocean waters is to reduce global emissions of carbon dioxide.

Melting Sea Ice Coloring Activity

Instructions

Use a blue pencil or crayon the color of the ocean to color the section between the sea ice and the ocean. Write this label on the section you colored, "**20 years ago this was sea ice**".

*Since 2000, the amount of Arctic sea ice has decreased by **50%**. There is less sea ice on Earth today than at any time on record.*

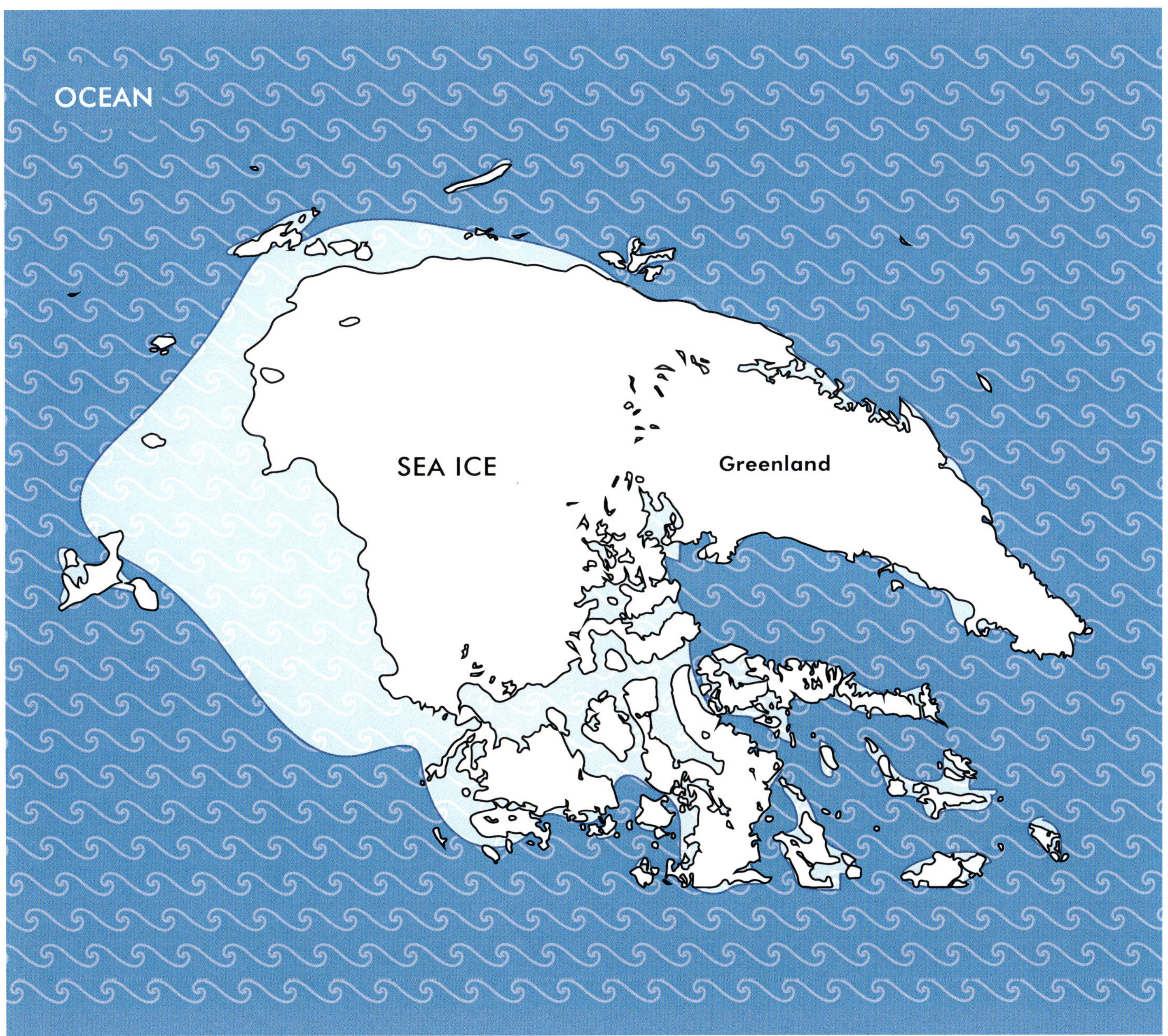

The Effect of the Rising Temperature on a Major Carbon Sink
Sinking Time into the Scientific Method

The ocean is a major carbon sink. Scientists estimate that the ocean has absorbed over half of all man-made carbon dioxide emissions. A **carbon sink** absorbs and stores more carbon dioxide from the atmosphere than it releases. Do changes in the ocean water's temperature affect the concentration of carbon dioxide in it? If there is an effect, does it cause a positive or a negative feedback loop, cycling more or less carbon dioxide into the atmosphere? With the understanding that global warming is happening globally and the knowledge that about 71 percent of Earth's surface is covered in water, with the world's oceans accounting for most of that water, do you think the effect (if there is any) will be local or global? Why not apply the scientific method to this and find out. To do that, you will need to form a hypothesis about the above questions, conduct an experiment where you collect data and make observations, and then analyze the data and think about the observations to form a conclusion.

For this experiment you will drop effervescent tablets into water at two different temperatures. As the effervescent tablets dissolve, gas bubbles will form. The bubbles observed coming from the tablets are made of carbon dioxide gas. Some of the gas will dissolve in the liquid and some will escape into the air. The amount of carbon dioxide gas that dissolves and remains in the water is a measure of the solubility of carbon dioxide gas in water at the temperature of the water. This experiment looks at how the solubility of carbon dioxide gas is affected by the temperature of water. (Answers pages 86 and 87.)

Materials

- 6 effervescent tablets
- 1 ½ L (or 6 cups) of water
- 2 thermometers
- 6 glasses
- Refrigerator
- Microwave or stove top for warming water
- The Effect of the Rising Temperature on a Major Carbon Sink lab sheet
- Paper
- Pen or pencil
- Camera: *Optional*
- Timer

Procedure

1. Write your hypothesis on The Effect of Rising Temperatures on a Major Carbon Sink lab sheet. Your hypothesis should answer the questions:
    a. Do changes in the temperature of water affect the solubility of carbon dioxide in it?
    b. If there is an effect, does it cause a positive or a negative feedback loop, cycling more or less carbon dioxide out of the water and into the atmosphere?
    c. If there is an effect, will the effect be local or global?
2. Put 750-mL (3 cups) water in a refrigerator for at least 1 hour. Before removing the water from the refrigerator, gently warm the 750-mL (3 cups) water that was not refrigerated to about 40°C (105°F).

3. Take the chilled water out of the refrigerator and measure its temperature. Record the temperature on the lab sheet.
4. Measure the temperature of the warmed water with the other thermometer. Record the temperature on the lab sheet.
5. Measure 250-mL (1 cup) of chilled water into each of three glasses for a total of 750-mL of water. Measure 250-mL (1 cup) of warm water into each of three glasses. Do this quickly so the water does not have time to warm or cool.
6. With the 6 glasses of water all in a row, quickly drop 1 effervescent tablet into each glass.
7. Set timer for 3 minutes. Every 1 minute, record your observations about the bubbling in each glass in the data table on the lab sheet. Take photos to include in the data section if you have a camera.
8. Set the timer for 15 minutes. Put the glasses of chilled water back into the refrigerator. Leave the other three sitting out. When the timer goes off, take the glasses out of the refrigerator and observe the amount of bubbles clinging to the inside of the glass below the water line for the warm and chilled water. Stir the solution in each glass at both temperatures, and hold it up to the light to see which still has more carbon dioxide bubbles. Use the amount of bubbles in the liquid that you observe for each temperature as an indication of solubility for carbon dioxide gas at the two different temperatures.
9. Complete the lab sheet.

The Effect of the Rising Temperature on a Major Carbon Sink Lab Sheet

Fill in the Lab Sheet as You Go Along.

Hypothesis:

Data Table: Recorded Observation for the Solubility of CO_2 in Warm and Chilled Water

TEMPERATURE		TEMPERATURE	
Chilled Water	**Observations about Solubility**	**Warm Water**	**Observations about Solubility**
Glass 1	**1.**	**Glass 1**	**1.**
	2.		**2.**
	3.		**3.**
Glass 2	**1.**	**Glass 2**	**1.**
	2.		**2.**
	3.		**3.**
Glass 3	**1.**	**Glass 3**	**1.**
	2.		**2.**
	3.		**3.**

The Effect of the Rising Temperature on a Major Carbon Sink Lab Sheet Continued

Solubility After 15 Minutes			
	OBSERVATIONS ABOUT SOLUBILITY		OBSERVATIONS ABOUT SOLUBILITY
Chilled Water	**1.**	**Warm Water**	**1.**
	2.		**2.**
	3.		**3.**

Conclusion: Analyze Your Data and Observations

How does the temperature of water affect the solubility of carbon dioxide in the water? Is carbon dioxide more soluble in warm water or chilled water?

Use the results from this experiment to draw real world conclusions.

How does the rising temperature of the world's oceans affect the solubility of carbon dioxide in them? Is this effect local or global?

Does it make the oceans a more or less effective carbon sink?

Do rising ocean temperatures create a negative or positive feedback loop cycling more or less carbon dioxide into the atmosphere? Draw a picture of this feedback loop below.

What Does it Matter if the Temperature Rises a Little?

Earth is 4,500,000,000 years old. The climate has changed many times during that time. You might be wondering what the problem is. So what if the temperature is hotter, it rains a little more or less, the sea level rises, or the ice sheets are thinner and smaller? All of these have happened in the past. What is the problem if they happen again?

The problem with the climate change that is happening now is the **rate** or speed that it is happening. Many plants and animals will not have time to **adapt**, adjust, to the new conditions.

For some organisms such as jelly fish, albatross, mosquitos, bark beetles, and many other insects, it isn't a problem.

The changing climate is a big problem for other organisms such as the pine trees that the bark beetles infest, penguins, and those that make and depend on coral reefs.

People are feeling some effects, too. Worldwide supplies of food and water are being affected. Coastal areas where people live are being swamped or flooded as the sea level rises. Infectious diseases such as malaria, West Nile virus, and Lyme Disease, are transmitted to people by mosquitos and ticks, respectively. These diseases are increasingly common as mosquito and tick populations thrive as the planet warms.

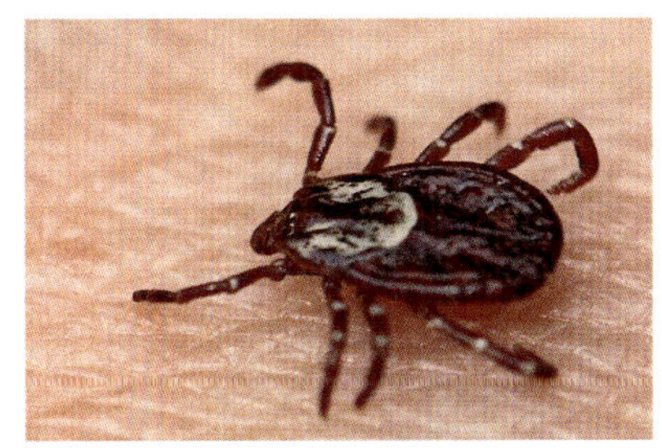

Many organisms, including humans, are sensitive to temperature. Did you know that humans are temperature sensitive? It's easy to forget, because humans live inside, and can turn on the heat, air conditioner, or a fan if it gets too cold or too warm. Humans can also take off and put on layers of clothes. Heat sensitivity is one of the reasons some organisms are struggling to adapt at the rate the climate is changing.

Most plants and animals do not have houses where they can turn up or down the temperature. Plants and animals can't take clothes off and put them on if they get warm or cold. Humans are sensitive to the temperature, but humans can control their environment to do something about it. Most species of organisms cannot control their environment. Without the ability to change their environment to help them cope, climate change can cause stress.

The evolution of new traits takes time. Under stressful conditions those species that need more time to adapt to the changing climate are at risk of extinction. **Extinction** happens when all the members of a species die, and there can never be any more of that type of plant or animal. Members of the same **species** are those organisms that can produce offspring that can then produce their own offspring. The rate of extinction is increasing as the rate of global warming and climate change increases.

All the bears in the world are not a species.

There are several species of bears.

All the bears that live in a certain area are not a species.

All the polar bears in the world are a species of bear. Polar bears are one of the species threatened with extinction because of global warming and climate change.

Adaptation Activity: It's All about the Rate

Scientists often use models to help understand how the natural and physical world works. A **scientific model** is a simplified representation of a real system. These models make it possible to study large, complex scientific principles and systems. Models can be simplified so that a single aspect of a complex situation is being looked at. This simple model gives a clear demonstration of how hard it can be to avoid an event that occurs at a fast rate. (Answers page 87.)

Materials

You will need a tennis ball (or another soft-type ball) and another person for this activity. Follow the instructions and answer the questions.

Procedure and Observations

1. Stand approximately 10 meters away from each other. Slowly roll the tennis ball to the other person. When the tennis ball gets close, but not until it is close, the other person to whom you rolled the ball should dodge out of the way of the ball. Next have him or her slowly roll the ball back to you. When the ball gets close to you, dodge out of the way of it. Was it easy or hard to avoid the ball at this slow rate?

2. Continue rolling the ball back and forth to each other, dodging to get away from it each time it gets close. Slowly increase the speed that you are rolling the ball. Each time you increase the speed of the ball, you are increasing the rate at which you are rolling the ball. Continue rolling the ball back and forth until you are both rolling it is as fast as you can. Don't forget to dodge out of the way each time the ball gets close. How was your ability to dodge out of the way of the ball affected as the rate it was coming toward you increased?

3. Answer the questions below. How do you think the increasing rate of climate change will affect the ability of some plants and animals to adapt?

   The organisms that are most at risk of extinction are those that have specialized needs and traits. This indicates organisms that need specific conditions to survive are struggling the most as the rate of climate change is increasing. Why do you think that is the case? (You can take your time to respond to this question if you need to. Perhaps, talk it over with another person and brainstorm the answer.)

   All this talk about adaptation might make you think people are not being affected by climate change. Use the internet to research how climate change and the rising sea levels caused by climate change are affecting people. Share your research with another person.

The increased concentration of greenhouse gas molecules in the air is enhancing the greenhouse effect. This enhanced greenhouse effect is causing global warming which is causing climate change.

PART 4: WHAT CAN BE DONE TO HELP?

The climate change happening now at the rate it is happening is caused by human activities. Humans caused this problem, so it's up to us to fix it. In 2013, there were 7.125 billion people on Earth. Today there are more than that. The problem with the increase in greenhouse gases doesn't come from one person burning a piece of paper, driving a car, or turning on a light. The problem occurs when more than 7.125 billion people do those things. People are pretty smart though. If EVERYONE came together to solve this problem, we could solve it.

Alternative Sources of Energy

One of the most important things humans can do is to burn less coal, gasoline, and oil. Burning those to make energy to power machines is the cause of the increased amounts of greenhouse gases going into the air. If you are thinking to yourself, "Wait a minute; we still are going to need things made by machines and to be able to drive and fly places." You are right, but there are alternative sources for energy. Alternative sources of energy are those that make electricity without releasing greenhouse gases. To slow the rate of climate change, people need to start investing in and using alternative sources of energy. Wind- and solar-generated energy are alternative sources of energy that generate energy without releasing greenhouses gases into the air.

Wind turbines use the wind to make energy. Solar panels use the sun to make energy. Energy made from the wind and sun does not release greenhouse gases into the air.

Hybrid and electric cars are much less polluting ways of driving. Hybrid cars release fewer greenhouse gases than gasoline-powered cars. Electric cars use electricity to run. Electric cars do not release carbon dioxide, methane, or nitrous oxide into the air when they are driven. If the electricity needed to power electric cars is produced by alternative energy sources, people can drive electric cars without releasing any greenhouse gases. Driving electric or hybrid vehicles helps slow global warming.

Comparing the Carbon "Tire"-Prints of Cars Activity

The cloud over each car gives information about how many grams of carbon dioxide is released for each mile that type of car is driven. The amounts are a measure of both the carbon dioxide in the exhaust from the cars (if there is any) and the carbon dioxide that is generated when the fuel is made. In the case of the electric car, when the electricity needed to charge the car is made, it was assumed that some natural gas and coal was used to generate the electricity. If solar and wind power are used to generate the electricity, the electric car will not release any carbon dioxide. These numbers are averages for a mid-sized sedan. (Answers page 87.)

Color the cloud over each car, and then answer the questions below.

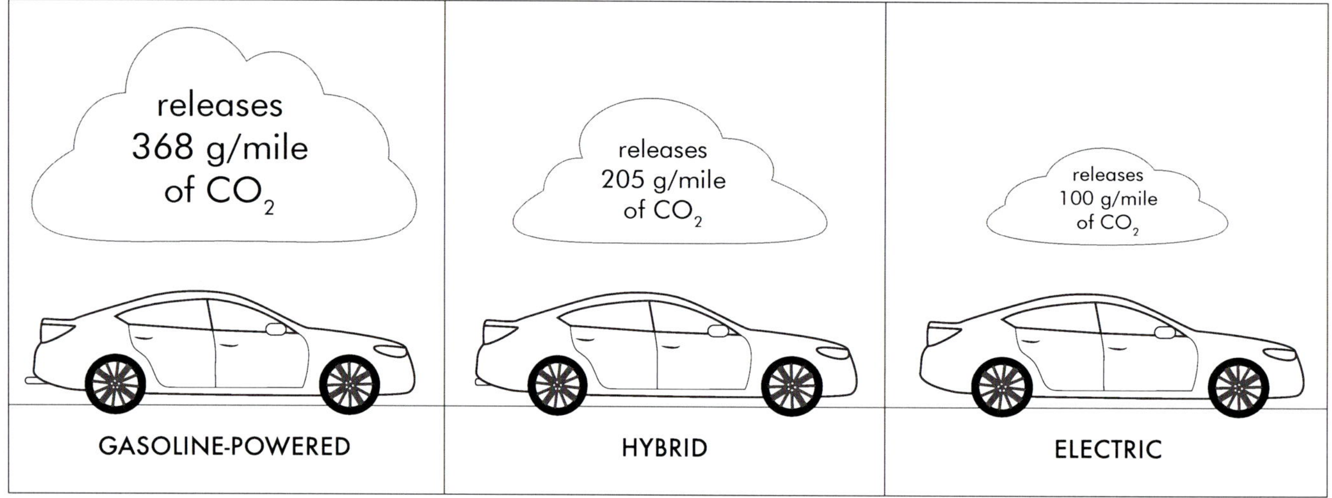

1. Use words and/or numbers to compare the amount of carbon dioxide released for each type of car.

2. Assume each car was driven 100 miles in a week. How much carbon dioxide would be released? (Hint: multiply the above numbers by 100.) As each car type drives more miles, how significant is the difference in the amount of carbon dioxide released for each type?

3. How would the amount of carbon dioxide released change for the electric car if all the electricity came from alternative energy sources?

These do not sound like things a kid can do to help fix this problem, do they? The good news is, there are things kids can do to help.

Your Carbon Footprint and How You Can Reduce It

How big are your feet? Even if they are really big, they don't make a footprint as large as your carbon footprint. Your **carbon footprint** is the amount of carbon dioxide and other carbon compounds emitted into the air because of your energy consumption. The more energy you use the larger your carbon footprint is, and the less energy you use the smaller your carbon footprint is. Some things that contribute to your carbon footprint are obvious. Driving, flying in a plane, cooking, and turning on lights all obviously use energy and add to the size of your carbon footprint.

Some contributions to your carbon footprint are not as obvious. Anything you use and consume that requires energy to make is also a part of your carbon footprint. Cookies from the grocery store, a new outfit, and a new toy all require energy to make and therefore are a part of your carbon footprint. The heat needed to warm water for your showers and wash your clothes is also part of your carbon footprint. Everything you use that is made by a machine, requires the use of a machine, or transported by a machine is a part of your carbon footprint.

To reduce your carbon footprint you need to use fewer things that required the burning of coal, gasoline, and oil.

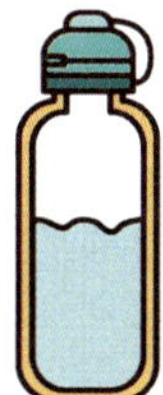

Stop Drinking Bottled Water

Bottled water has a big carbon footprint. Plastic bottles take energy to make. It takes energy to get the water from its source into the bottle. Energy is also required to transport the bottles of water. A much better solution is to drink from reusable containers.

Turn Off the Lights

It turns out your parents are right. You should turn off the lights. It might seem like a little thing to remember. If over 7.125 billion people worked together to remember to turn off the lights, it would make a big difference.

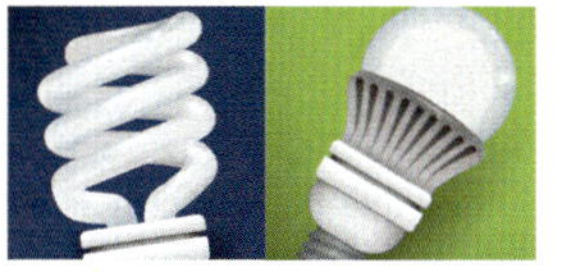

Change to New Energy Efficient Light Bulbs

CFL and LED light bulbs use only 20 to 25% of the energy that traditional, incandescent, bulbs use.

Walk More, Drive Less

Cars emit greenhouse gases. Instead of driving, walk or ride your bike or skateboard to get places. It is great exercise and good for the planet.

Explain Global Warming and Climate Change to Another Person

Sharing knowledge with others is a great way to enact change. People need to understand the science of global warming and climate change in order to understand changes they can make to help fix the situation.

The Foods You Eat

Food choices can make a difference to the size of your carbon footprint. Most food bought at the grocery store is processed and cooked at a factory. Before that, the raw materials for the food are transported to the factory. After the food is processed, machines package the food. Once the food is packaged, trucks deliver the food to stores. Some foods, especially those that are pre-made and have to be delivered from distant locations, have a big carbon footprint.

Choosing foods from sources near you or that you make or grow at home makes your carbon footprint smaller.

Homemade foods don't have to be delivered or packaged.

Eat local.

Start a garden.

Eat Less Meat

Meat has a larger carbon footprint than any other commonly eaten type of food. That is because animals require food to be grown for them and fed to them. The food these animals eat has a carbon footprint. Plant based foods have a lower carbon footprint than other types of food, because plants need only the sun, water, and carbon dioxide. (That's right, plants use carbon dioxide from the air to grow.)

Food Has a Carbon Footprint: Field Trip to the Grocery Store

Did you know that many ingredients in pet food come from China? Ingredients in chocolate often come from Africa. Fresh fruit and vegetables in the middle of winter most likely come from far away. The food your family eats comes from all over the world. The farther food travels before being eaten, the larger the carbon footprint is for that food. You are going to take a trip to the local grocery store, or the pantry in your kitchen, to investigate where the foods you like to eat come from and get some information about the carbon footprint of those foods.

You will need the Field Trip to the Grocery Store Worksheet in Appendix 3, a ride to the store, a pen or pencil, and an atlas or access to the internet.

Food Has a Carbon Footprint: Field Trip to the Grocery Store: Continued

Food packaging gives information about where food comes from. Often the information is not complete. For example, you might learn where your favorite cookies are made, but not where the flour, sugar, and eggs used to make the cookies came from. Even without that information, you'll learn something about the carbon footprint of your favorite foods.

Procedure

1. Drive to the grocery store or walk into your kitchen to look at the labels of your favorite food.
2. Fill in the sections of this worksheet with locations where the food is made, grown, or packaged. You cannot always get all of this information. You can use a pen and pencil to write this down or you can use your phone and take pictures of it, and then record your answers on the worksheet at home.
3. Fresh fruits and vegetables have labels on them telling where the food is grown and therefore transported from. Packaged food has information about where the food comes from below the label stating the Nutrition Facts.
4. When you're finished, use an atlas or your computer to fill in column three of the table to get a rough estimate of how far your favorite food has traveled. The distance does not need to be exact. If you live in Colorado and you love avocados, and you learn that avocados at this time of year come from Mexico, you do not need to know exactly where in Mexico to get a rough estimate of how far the avocados have traveled.
5. If you do not have favorite foods in one of the categories, choose foods in that category to determine what the carbon footprint is for a food in that category.
6. Answer the questions after the worksheet has been filled out.

Questions

What items of food came from farthest away?

Were you surprised by the distances any of the food items traveled? If yes, which foods surprised you the most? Why was it surprising?

Many of your favorite foods are made from multiple ingredients. Those raw ingredients for those foods have to be brought to a processing plant where the food is then made. Now that you know about the carbon footprint of some of the raw ingredients, such as fruits and vegetables, eggs, milk, or meat, what can you say about the carbon footprint of packaged food compared to food items that are a single ingredient item? For example, an apple or eggs are a single ingredient item.

How could you use the information you learned about the carbon footprint of your favorite foods to reduce your carbon footprint?

Reduce, Reuse, Recycle

Reducing, reusing, and recycling are the three R's for helping Earth. When you reduce and reuse things instead of buying new, machines work less, using less energy, which leads to lower amounts of greenhouse gases being put in the air and a smaller carbon footprint.

REDUCE

REUSE

RECYCLE

Trees are cut down to make paper. Oil, natural gas, and coal are refined to make plastic. Aluminum and other metals are mined to get the materials to make metal products. It takes machines to get these materials and to make the paper, plastics, and metal products. When you recycle, you eliminate the step where these materials are gathered and changed from the raw materials.

Recycling also keeps materials, like paper, out of **landfills** and **dumps**. These are where trash is disposed of after it leaves your house. At landfills and dumps, paper products begin to decompose. When they do, they release methane into the air. When you recycle paper, less energy is used to make new paper products, and less of the greenhouse gas methane is emitted into the air at landfills as the paper decomposes!

Paper and plant materials in this landfill are decomposing. As they decompose, they release methane into the air.

Composting recycles organic material to make fertilizer.

Recycling paper products and composting fruit and vegetable scraps reduces the methane coming from landfills and dumps. **Composting** is the process of allowing organic materials, like coffee grounds, banana peels, and eggshells, to decay to use as fertilizer. When materials decompose in a compost versus at the landfill, they release less greenhouse gas.

Why Recycle?

This graph compares the amount of five different products that can be made from unrecycled material versus recycled material using the same amount of energy.

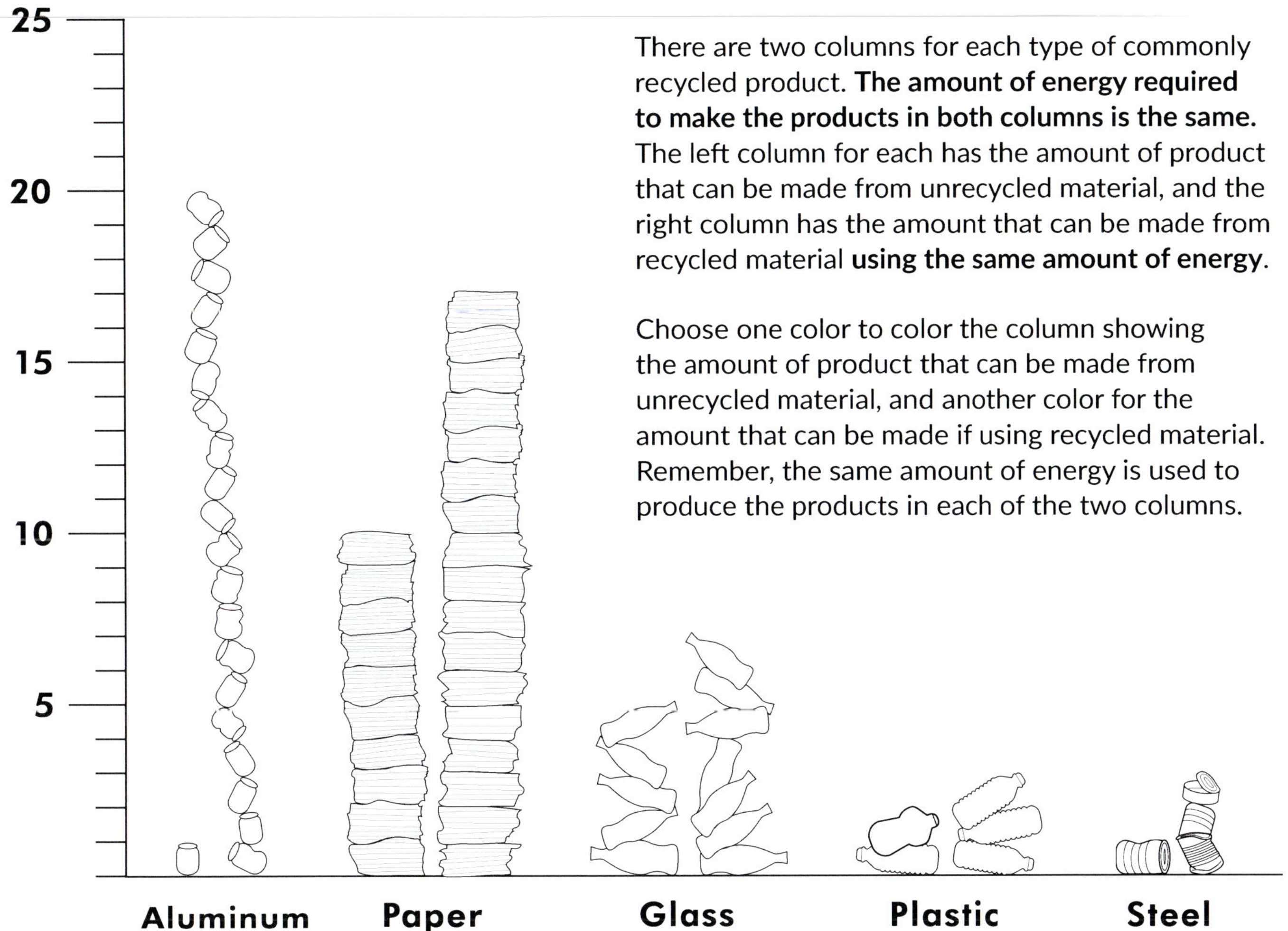

There are two columns for each type of commonly recycled product. **The amount of energy required to make the products in both columns is the same.** The left column for each has the amount of product that can be made from unrecycled material, and the right column has the amount that can be made from recycled material **using the same amount of energy**.

Choose one color to color the column showing the amount of product that can be made from unrecycled material, and another color for the amount that can be made if using recycled material. Remember, the same amount of energy is used to produce the products in each of the two columns.

Follow the instructions to complete the graph, and then answer the questions below and on the next page.

Label each column. The left column for each type of product should be labeled "Unrecycled" or "U." and the right column for each type of product should be labeled "Recycled" or "R."

Count the number of items in each column, and write the number for products made from unrecycled materials to that made from recycled materials in the table below. (Answers page 88.)

The Amount of Product That Can Be Made from Unrecycled Material Versus Recycled Material Using the Same Amount of Energy									
Alumunum U	Alumunum R	Paper U	Paper R	Glass U	Glass R	Plastic U	Plastic R	Steel U	Steel R

Using the same amount of energy, how many new aluminum cans can be made from unrecycled versus recycled aluminum?

Using the same amount of energy, how much new paper can be made from unrecycled versus recycled paper?

Using the same amount of energy, how much new glass can be made from unrecycled versus recycled glass?

Using the same amount of energy, how much new plastic can be made from unrecycled versus recycled plastic?

Using the same amount of energy, how many new steel cans can be made from unrecycled versus recycled steel cans?

Which type of material saves the most energy to recycle? Circle the correct answer.

Aluminum Paper Glass Plastic Steel

In one to two sentences explain how recycling saves energy.

In one to two sentences, explain the benefits of recycling instead of having materials go to dumps and landfills.

How I Am Going to Shrink My Carbon Footprint and Help Stop Global Warming

Now you know some of the simple ways you can shrink your carbon footprint and help combat global warming and climate change. In the space below, write what you are going to do to help.

1.

2.

3.

4.

5.

6.

7.

8.

9.

10.

IF **EVERYONE** COMES TOGETHER TO SOLVE THIS PROBLEM, WE CAN SOLVE IT.

COMPOST

EAT LOCAL, AND EAT LESS MEAT

HOMEMADE FOOD

TURN OFF THE LIGHTS

REUSABLE WATER BOTTLES

RECYCLE

REUSE

WALK, RIDE, OR SKATEBOARD INSTEAD OF DRIVING

GARDEN

USE ALTERNATIVE SOURCES OF ENERGY INSTEAD OF COAL, OIL, AND GASOLINE

BIBLIOGRAPHY

Butler, James H., and Stephen A. Montzka. *The NOAA Annual Greenhouse Gas Index (AGGI).* NO_2. NOAA. Retrieved from: https://www.esrl.noaa.gov/gmd/aggi/aggi.html

Carbon Dioxide, Methane, and Nitrous Oxide IR Spectrums. NIST Chemistry WebBook. Retrieved from: http://webbook.nist.gov/chemistry

Car Emission Statistics. Retrieved from: http://www.fueleconomy.gov/feg/Find.do?action=sbsSelect

Dahlman, LuAnn. *Percent Warming of Ocean*. NOAA. Retrieved from: https://www.climate.gov/news-features/understanding-climate/climate-change-ocean-heat-content

Dlugokencky, Ed. NOAA /ESRL. *Recent Global* CH_4. Retrieved from: http://esrl.noaa.gov/gmd/ccgg/trends_ch4

Dlugokencky, Ed, and Tans, Pieter. NOAA /ESRL. *Recent Monthly Average Mauna Loa.* CO_2. Retrieved from: http://esrl.noaa.gov/gmd/ccgg/trends

How Energy Efficient Light Bulbs Compare with Traditional. Retrieved from: https://energy.gov/energysaver/how-energy-efficient-light-bulbs-compare-traditional-incandescents

Ma, Qiancheng. *Temperature of Earth without Greenhouse Effect*. NASA. Retrieved from: https://www.giss.nasa.gov/research/briefs/ma_01

NOAA National Centers for Environmental Information. *State of the Climate: Global Climate Report for Annual 2016*. Retrieved from: https://www.ncdc.noaa.gov/sotc/global/201613

Tans. Pieter, and Thoning, Kirk. *Mole Fraction in Dry Air*. NOAA Earth System Research Laboratory. Retrieved from: https://www.esrl.noaa.gov/gmd/ccgg/about/co2_measurements.html

Graphs

NOAA: 36, 40, 41.

NASA: 31, 38.

Photos

NASA: 31.

Stacy Hargrove for NOAA: 48.

NOAA: 50.

IR Spectrum

NIST: 31.

LIST OF SUPPLIES

This list has the supplies you will need. If an item has been listed one time, it is not listed again, even if it is used in a later lab.

- ☐ Scissors
- ☐ Tape
- ☐ Pen or pencil
- ☐ Water
- ☐ Sugar
- ☐ Drink mix, like Kool-Aid
- ☐ Ice
- ☐ Pitcher
- ☐ Measuring cup
- ☐ 1/4 teaspoon measuring spoon
- ☐ Black construction paper
- ☐ Timer (the one on your phone works great)
- ☐ 2 Drinking glasses
- ☐ 2 Thermometers
- ☐ Plastic wrap
- ☐ Paper
- ☐ Matches
- ☐ Car that is not an electric car
- ☐ Light switch that turns on a light
- ☐ Calculator
- ☐ Internet access
- ☐ Blue pencil or crayon
- ☐ 6 Effervescent tablets
- ☐ 6 Drinking glasses
- ☐ Refrigerator
- ☐ Microwave or stove top for warming water
- ☐ Camera: *Optional*
- ☐ Tennis ball
- ☐ Another person
- ☐ A colored pencil or crayon in a color other than blue

APPENDIX 1: HOW MANY MOLECULES ARE IN A BOX OF AIR TEMPLATE

Procedure

1. Tear out this page with the template below or make a copy of it.
2. Cut along the outside of the template. Do not cut where there are dotted lines.
3. After you have cut the template out, fold each square flap at the dotted line. Be careful not to rip the flaps.
4. Before folding up the sides, write "8 cubic centimeters" or "8 cm^3" on one of the sides that will be on the outside of the box.
5. Fold each side to make a cube.
6. Tape or glue the edges so that the cube stays together.
7. When you have finished making the box go back to page 9. Do not peek at page 10 until you have made a guess about how many gas molecules are in the box.

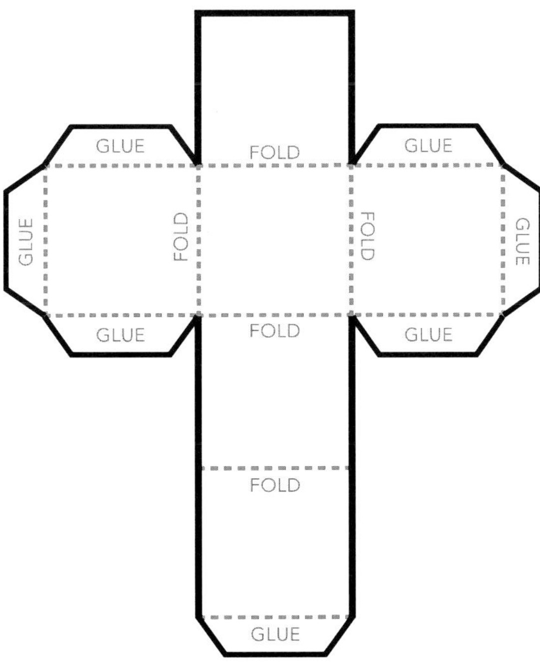

Concentration Data for Greenhouse Gases from 2000 to 2018

Carbon Dioxide, CO_2 Concentration Data in Parts per Million		Methane, CH_4 Concentration Data in Parts per Million		Nitrous Oxide, N_2O Concentration Data in Parts per Million	
2000	370	2000	1.773	2000	0.316
2001	371	2001	1.771	2001	0.317
2002	373	2002	1.773	2002	0.317
2003	376	2003	1.777	2003	0.318
2004	378	2004	1.777	2004	0.318
2005	380	2005	1.774	2005	0.319
2006	382	2006	1.775	2006	0.320
2007	384	2007	1.781	2007	0.321
2008	386	2008	1.787	2008	0.322
2009	387	2009	1.793	2009	0.322
2010	390	2010	1.799	2010	0.323
2011	392	2011	1.803	2011	0.325
2012	394	2012	1.808	2012	0.325
2013	397	2013	1.813	2013	0.326
2014	399	2014	1.822	2014	0.328
2015	401	2015	1.834	2015	0.329
2016	404	2016	1.843	2016	0.330
2017	407	2017	1.858	2017	0.331
2018	409	2018	1.863	2018	0.332
2019	410	2019	1.875	2019	0.333

APPENDIX 3: FIELD TRIP TO THE GROCERY STORE WORKSHEET

FOOD TYPE	WHERE IT CAME FROM	HOW FAR THAT IS FROM MY HOUSE
Fruits and Vegetables		
Packaged Foods		
Foods in the Dairy Aisle		
Candy		
Bread		
Meat or Meat Substitutes		
Drinks Including Bottled Water		
Pet Food		

APPENDIX 4: ANSWER KEY

Page 9: How Many Are There in a Box of Air, Continued

200,000,000,000,000,000,000 = 2.0 x 10^{20}
Answers will vary for the last two questions, but the answers should be large numbers.

Page 11: Can you find the four most common types of atoms that make air: N, O, Ar, and C?

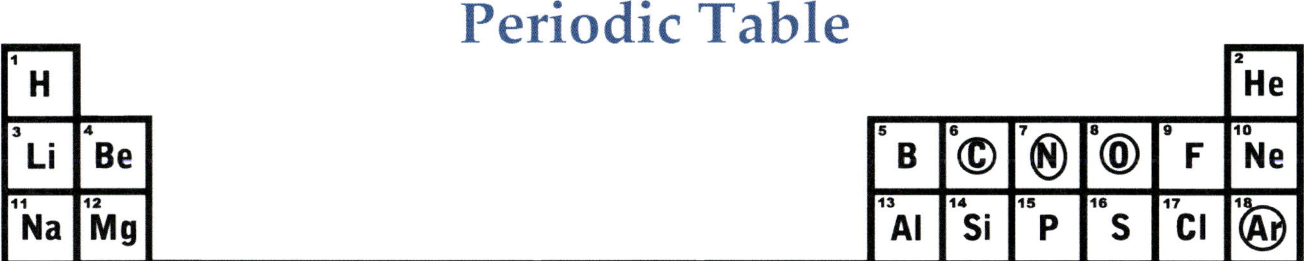

Page 13: How Small Amounts Can Have a Big Effect

1. How does the water taste? What color is the water? How does the water smell? **There is no taste. The color is clear. There is no smell.**
2. Did adding the sugar to the water change the taste? Did it change the color? Does the water smell different? **The taste changed, but the color and smell did not. This might vary if using raw sugar.**
3. How did adding ice to the sugar-water mix change the taste? Did the color change? Did the smell change? The atoms argon and neon are sometimes called inert gases. What does inert mean? **The ice did not change the taste, color, or smell. Inert means chemically inactive.**
4. Based on the measurement from the cup, how much drink mix was in the packet? **Slightly less than 1/2 ounce**
5. How do the taste, smell, and color change after each addition? **After each addition, the taste and smell became stronger, and the color darkened.**
6. Why was water chosen to model nitrogen gas? **Most of the molecules in the air are nitrogen, and most of the drink mix is made of water.**
7. Why was sugar chosen to model oxygen gas? **The second largest concentration of molecules in the air is oxygen, and the second largest concentration for an ingredient in this mix is sugar.**
8. Why were ice cubes chosen to model argon and neon? **Argon and neon added together are the 3rd most common component of air and ice is the 3rd most common component of the drink I made.**
9. Why was the drink mix chosen to model the molecules carbon dioxide, methane, and nitrous oxide? What do you think would happen if you increased the amount of drink mix? **The drink mix and the gas molecules, carbon dioxide, methane, and nitrous oxide, are in small concentrations in the mixes they are in. The amount of drink mix was just right. Increasing the amount of drink mix would make the taste too strong.**

Page 16: Absorbing the Sun's Energy Activity

Do you feel heat radiating from the paper? **No**

Now that the paper has been in the sunlight, do you feel more or less heat radiating from it? **More**

The molecules in the paper absorb energy from the sun and radiate it as heat to your hand. Draw a quick illustration of the process that occurs at the paper. Draw the energy from the sun and the heat that radiates from the paper as waves.

Do the molecules in paper radiate more or less heat when the paper is out of direct sunlight? Why do you think that is? **When the paper is taken out of the sun, it is removed from the energy source that caused it to heat. The heat radiated away from the paper, and the paper cooled, because there is no new heat energy being transferred to the paper.**

Page 18: How Many Molecules Are in Eight Cubic Centimeters of Dry Air

How Many Molecules Are in Eight Cubic Centimeters of Dry Air	Chemical Formula
157,800,000,000,000,000,000 (1.578×10^{20}) nitrogen gas molecules	N_2
41,880,000,000,000,000,000 (4.188×10^{19}) oxygen gas molecules	O_2
1,860,000,000,000,000,000 (1.86×10^{18}) argon gas molecules	Ar
81,800,000,000,000,000 (8.18×10^{16}) carbon dioxide gas molecules	CO_2
3,600,000,000,000,000 (3.6×10^{15}) neon gas molecules	Ne
372,600,000,000,000 (3.726×10^{14}) methane gas molecules	CH_4
66,400,000,000,000 (6.64×10^{13}) nitrous oxide gas molecules	N_2O

Page 19: Vibrating Molecules Heat Things Up The Greenhouse Effect Lab

Hypothesis: How will the temperature vary in the enclosed space versus the open space? **Answers may vary. At this point, however, students should suspect that there will be a larger temperature difference from start to finish for the temperature in the enclosed space as the greenhouse gases for that setup transfer heat energy from the sun to the air without a way for the heat to escape.**

Recording Data: Time 0 is when you begin recording data.

Time, minutes	Temperature, °C Enclosed Space	Temperature, °C Open Space
0	33	33
5	38	33
10	43	33
15	46	34
20	48	34
25	50	35
30	52	34

Temperature versus Time for the Air in an Enclosed Space and an Open Space

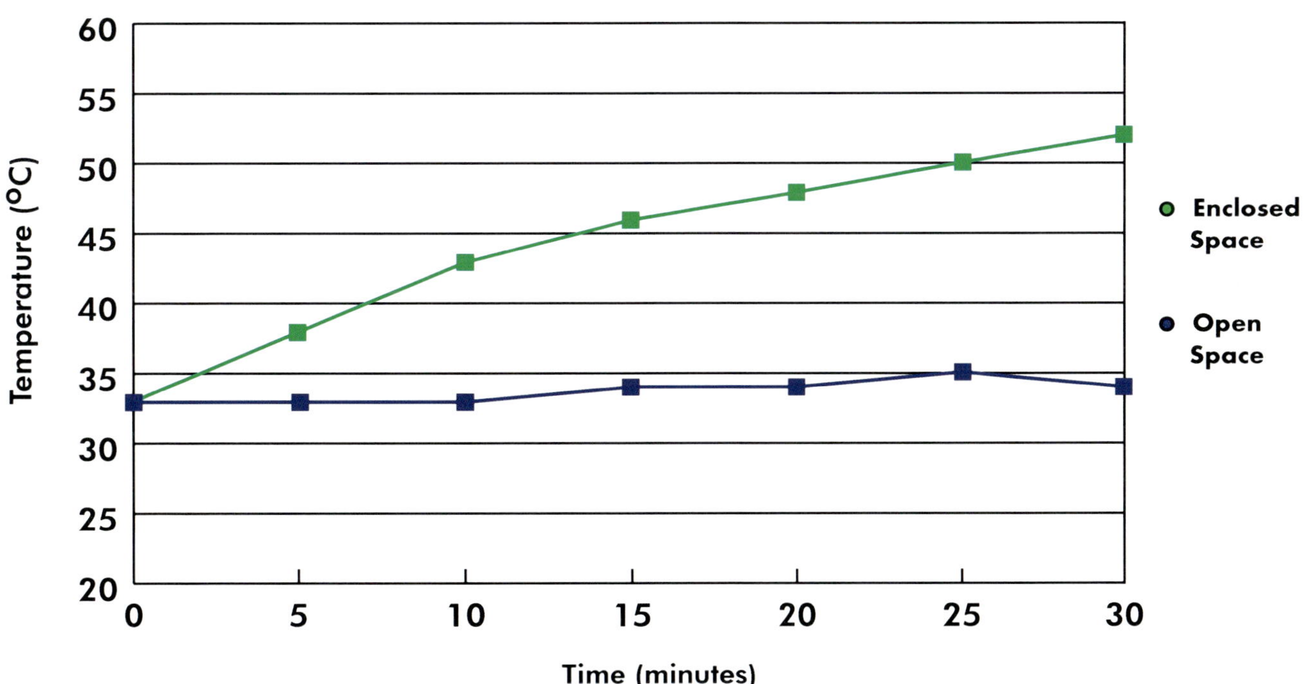

What is present in both glasses? **Air**

Were greenhouse gas molecules in both glasses? **Yes**

If yes, do you think the same concentration of greenhouse gas molecules is in both glasses? **Yes**

What was the main difference between the two setups? **The glass with the plastic wrap trapped the air and heat the greenhouse gas molecules were radiating into the air. The glass that was open to the air also had greenhouse gas molecules in it, but the gases and heat were not trapped in the glass.**

Vibrating Molecules Heat Things Up The Greenhouse Effect Lab *(Continued)*

Describe what you observed for the temperature curves for the two setups, both the enclosed space and the open space. **The curve for the enclosed space curved steadily up as the temperature of the air enclosed inside the glass increased. The curve for the open space was fairly flat.**

Use what you have learned to explain what you observed. **The air in the glass that was not enclosed was free to leave and enter the glass as the molecules moved around. In addition, the heat the greenhouse gas molecules radiated was able to radiate out of the glass. When the greenhouse gas molecules in the enclosed glass radiated heat, the heat was trapped from leaving the glass.**

Did your hypothesis do a good job of predicting what you observed? Why or why not? **Yes it did. I predicted there would be a larger difference in temperature increase for the air in the glass that was enclosed, because the heat would not be able to escape the glass.**

If the amount of greenhouse gases increased in the glass that was enclosed what would you expect to happen? **I would expect the temperature to be higher at time = 0 and increase at a faster rate.**

What if the amount decreased? **I would expect the temperature to be lower at time = 0 and increase at a slower rate.**

Page 24: Machine-Made or Not Activity: **Answers will vary**

Page 26: In the Name of Science: An Activity Where You Generate Greenhouse Gases

Oil, gasoline, paper, or coal (all or any one of these is correct) + oxygen gas ➔ greenhouse gases or carbon dioxide, nitrous oxide, and methane (either is correct) + water + energy

Page 27: Time for Some Math: How Many More?:

How Many More Are in Your Box: Either of the two styles for reporting the number are okay for this.

25,800,000,000,000,000 (**2.58×10^{16}**) carbon dioxide gas molecules

224,600,000,000,000 (**2.246×10^{14}**) methane gas molecules

13,800,000,000,000 (**1.38×10^{13}**) nitrous oxide gas molecules

Page 30: Graph the Concentrations of Greenhouse Gases

The answers for version A and B are the same.

Graph the Greenhouse Gases Answer Key

The projected point for the year 2020 on each graph should be higher on the graph than the point for 2019.

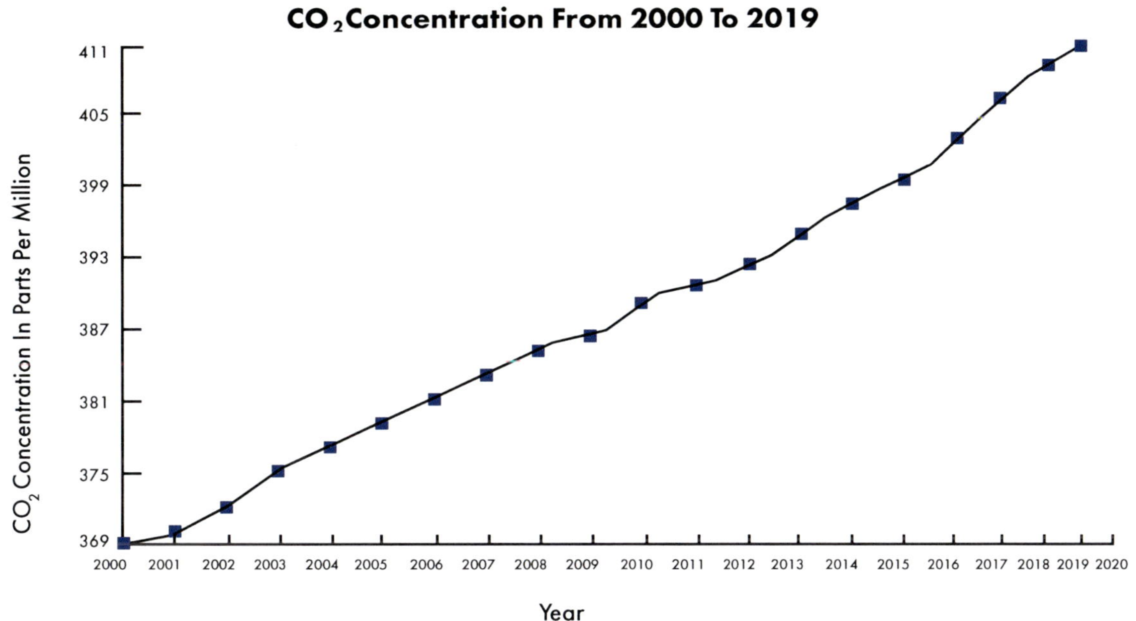

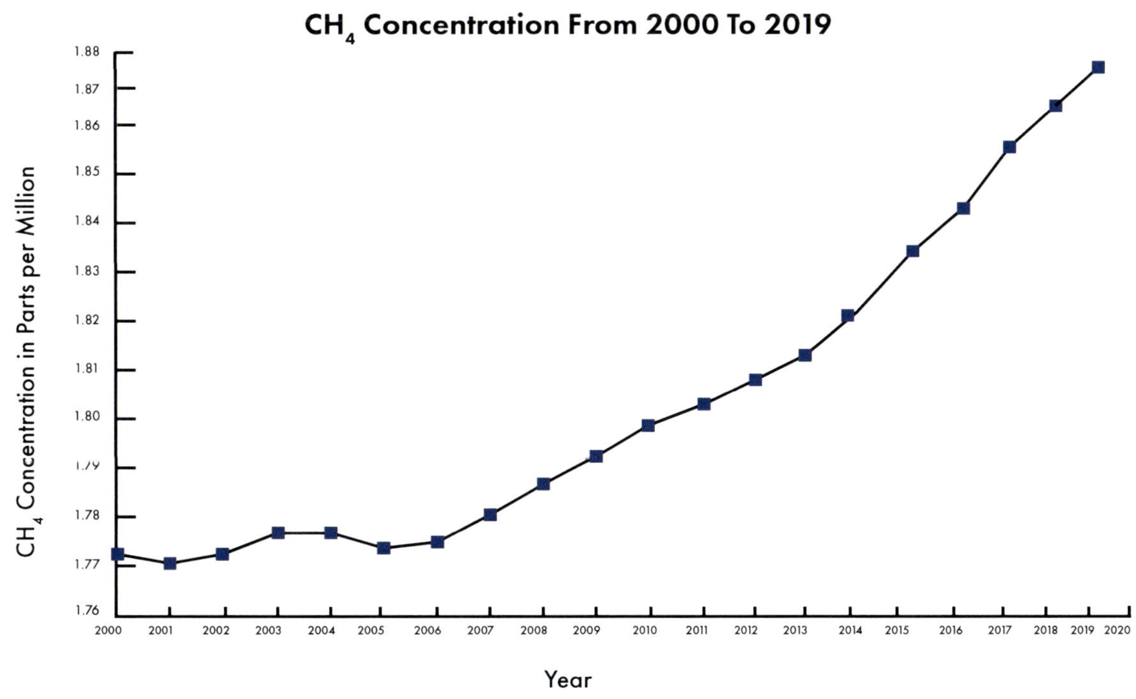

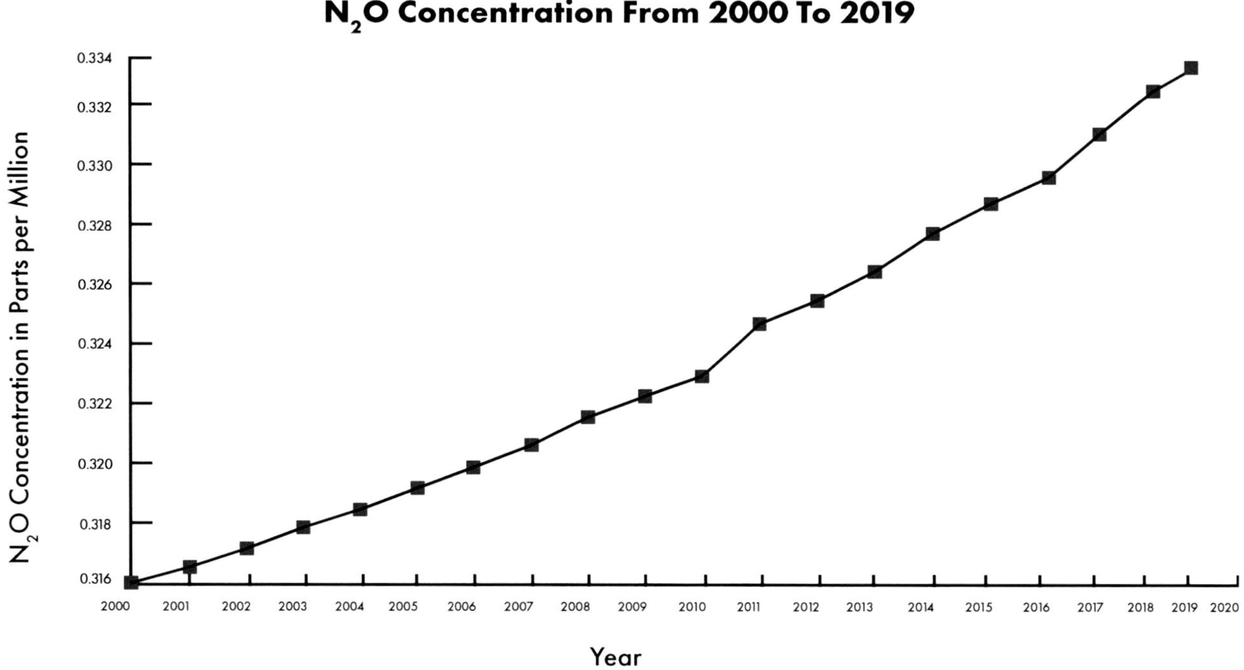

Are the concentrations of the three greenhouse gases increasing or decreasing?
They are increasing.

Do you think the concentration of these gases will increase or decrease over the next several years?
Based on the trend over the past 19 years, I expect them to continue increasing.

With the understanding that these gases trap the sun's energy and heat the air by radiating energy as heat, do you conclude that the average global temperature will increase, decrease, or stay the same? Give an explanation for your conclusion.
I expect the temperature to increase, because the concentration of greenhouse gas molecules which trap energy that heats the planet has increased.

Page 39: A Positive Feedback Loop for Methane

The Temperature Increases.

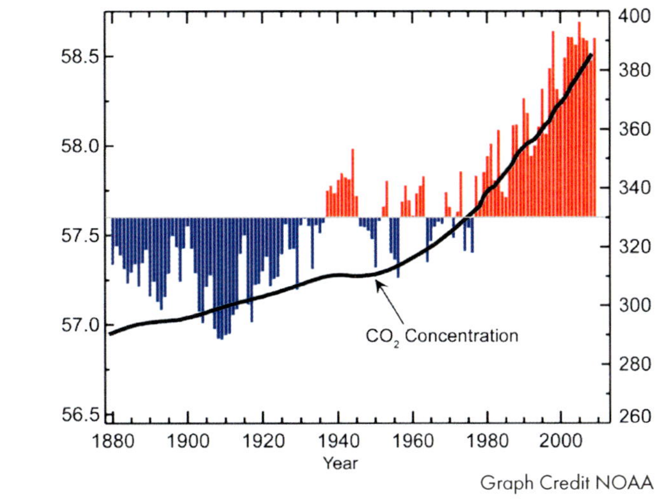

Graph Credit NOAA

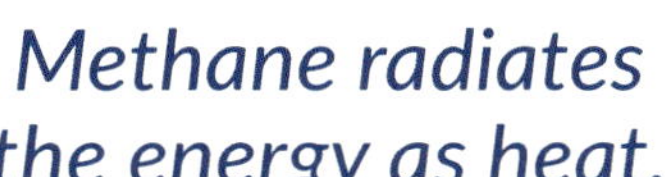

Methane radiates the energy as heat.

Permafrost melts.

Methane trapped beneath the permafrost is released into the air (atmosphere).

Methane absorbs energy from the sun.

Page 41: The Weather: What was the weather outside your house yesterday?

Answers will vary

Page 43: The Climate: What Has the Weather Been at My House for the Past 30 Years?

These are my answers for Nome, Alaska done for April 1, spanning the years 2017 to 1988. This is just an example. If you need to, you can use this data for your data set. This activity is a bit time-consuming, but it does a very effective job of demonstrating the difference between climate and weather.

The answers for this are on the next 2 pages.

Weather measurements for Nome, Alaska for April 1			
Year	Actual Mean Temperature	Precipitation	Wind Speed
2017	-7 °C	0 cm	11 kph
2016	-3 °C	3.814 cm	27 kph
2015	-17 °C	0 cm	2 kph
2014	-4 °C	0 cm	26 kph
2013	-15 °C	0 cm	5 kph
2012	-14 °C	0 cm	5 kph
2011	-14 °C	4.42 cm	18 kph
2010	-7 °C	0 cm	15 kph
2009	-15 °C	0.25 cm	5 kph
2008	-1 °C	0.15 cm	24 kph
2007	-1 °C	0.28 cm	16 kph
2006	-10 °C	0 cm	16 kph
2005	-14 °C	0 cm	3 kph
2004	-20 °C	0 cm	6 kph
2003	-3 °C	0.15 cm	16 kph
2002	-4 °C	0 cm	8 kph
2001	-15 °C	0 cm	13 kph
2000	-19 °C	0 cm	3 kph
1999	-12 °C	0 cm	24 kph
1998	-4 °C	0 cm	15 kph
1997	-19 °C	0 cm	5 kph
1996	-3 °C	0.71 cm	7 kph
1995	-3 °C	0.3 cm	8 kph
1994	-1 °C	0 cm	21 kph
1993	2 °C	1.88 cm	18 kph
1992	-18 °C	0 cm	5 kph
1991	-4 °C	0 cm	19 kph
1990	-14 °C	0 cm	6 kph
1989	-13 °C	0 cm	5 kph
1988	-13 °C	0 cm	23 kph

Climate measurements for Nome, Alaska for April 1
Temperature: -272÷30 = **-9.1 °C**
Precipitation: 11.32 ÷30 = **0.38 cm**
Wind Speed: 375÷30 = **12.5 kph**

1-Day Weather Measurements	30-Year Climate Measurements
-4 °C	**-9.1 °C**
0 cm	**0.38 cm**
11 kph	**12.5 kph**

The Climate: What Has the Weather Been at My House for the Past 30 Years? *(Continued)*

Use words to describe how the 1-day measurements compare with the 30-year averages. **The temperature is 5.1 degrees higher than expected. There was no precipitation yesterday, even though based on the average a small amount was expected. The wind measurement is very similar for weather and climate.**

What was the highest actual mean temperature recorded at your location during the past 30 years?

2 °C

What was the lowest actual mean temperature recorded at your location during the past 30 years?

-20 °C

What was the most amount of precipitation recorded at your location during the past 30 years?

4.42 cm

What was the least amount of precipitation recorded at your location during the past 30 years?

0 cm

What was the speed of the calmest wind speed recorded at your location during the past 30 years?

2 kph

What was the speed of the strongest wind speed recorded at your location during the past 30 years?

27 kph

To predict the weather for yesterday's date a year from now, would you use the climate measurements or the weather measurements? Give a reason for you choice. **I would use the 30-year average. The average is based on 30 measurements, 30 data sets, averaged together. The single-day measurement consists of just 1 data set. I can see from looking at the values on the Data Table for Climate that the numbers can range quite a bit from the average. When making a prediction it is better to base the prediction on an average than on a single measurement.**

Page 50: The Effect of the Rising Temperature on a Major Carbon Sink Lab Sheet

Hypothesis: Answers to the following questions will vary, but the hypothesis should include answers to all three questions. Do changes in the temperature of water affect the solubility of carbon dioxide in it? If there is an effect, does it cause a positive or a negative feedback loop, cycling more or less carbon dioxide into the atmosphere? If there is an effect, will the effect be local or global?

Data Table: Recorded Observation for the Solubility of CO_2 in Warm and Chilled Water			
	TEMPERATURE		TEMPERATURE
Chilled Water	3 °C	Warm Water	37 °C
	Observations about Solubility		Observations about Solubility
Glass 1	1. slow fizzing; stays on bottom	Glass 1	1. floated to top right away
	2. not fully dissolved yet		2. fully dissolved after 1 minute
	3. lots of bubbles on top; still not fully dissolved		3. there are bubbles but not as many
Glass 2	1. slow fizzing; stays on bottom	Glass 2	1. floated to top right away
	2. not fully dissolved yet		2. fully dissolved after 1 minute
	3. lots of bubbles on top; still not fully dissolved		3. there are bubbles but not as many
Glass 3	1. slow fizzing; stays on bottom	Glass 3	1. floated to top right away
	2. not fully dissolved yet		2. fully dissolved after 1 minute
	3. lots of bubbles on top; still not fully dissolved		3. there are bubbles but not as many

Solubility After 10 Minutes			
	OBSERVATIONS ABOUT SOLUBILITY		OBSERVATIONS ABOUT SOLUBILITY
Chilled Water	Had lots of small bubbles when I stirred the glasses. There was still carbon dioxide gas dissolved in the water.	Warm Water	Had some bigger bubbles clinging to the sides of the glass. When I stirred the mix these bubbles escaped into the air.

How does the temperature of water affect the solubility of carbon dioxide in the water? Is carbon dioxide more soluble in warm water or chilled water? Is this effect local or global? **Carbon dioxide is less soluble in warm water than it is in chilled water. Global.**

How does the rising temperature of the world's oceans affect the solubility of carbon dioxide in them? Is this effect local or global? **As ocean waters warm, carbon dioxide gas dissolved in it will escape the water and go into the air. Global.**

Does it make the oceans a more or less effective carbon sink? **It makes the oceans a less effective carbon sink.**

Do rising ocean temperatures create a negative or positive feedback loop cycling more or less carbon dioxide into the atmosphere? Draw a picture of this feedback loop.

Loops may vary.

Here is one possible loop.

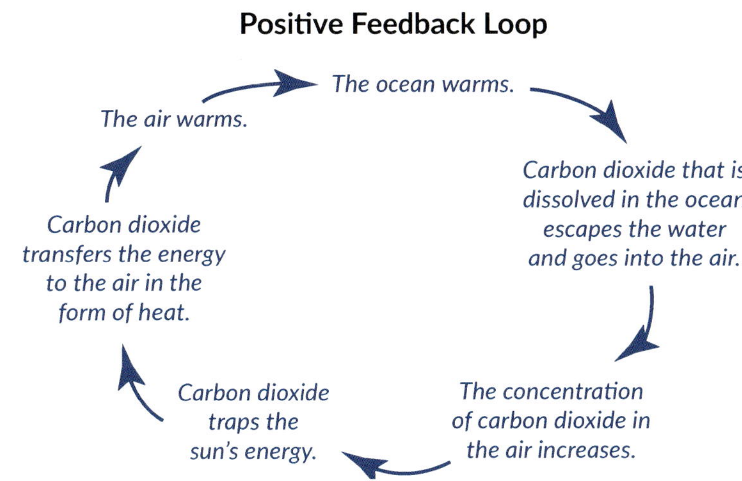

Page 55:Adaptation Activity: It's all about the Rate

Was it easy or hard to avoid the ball at this slow rate? How is your ability to dodge out of the way of the tennis ball affected as the rate it is coming toward you increases? **It becomes harder to get out of the way as the rate of speed increases. At a slow rate it is easy to dodge the tennis ball, as the rate increases it is harder to do.**

How do you think the increasing rate of climate change will affect the ability of some plants and animals to adapt to the change? **Some plants and animals will not be able to adapt to the changes in the climate, and they will go extinct.**

The organisms that need specific conditions to survive are struggling most as the rate of climate change is increasing. Why do you think that is the case? **It takes time for new traits to evolve. If a species needs to evolve in order to survive conditions that are changing because of climate change, there is less time for this to happen as the rate of change speeds up. This makes it less likely that new traits will evolve n time to save the species. Organisms with specialized needs have a more limited range of what they can tolerate to survive in the changing conditions.**

Page 58: Comparing the Carbon "Tire"-Prints of Cars Activity

1. Use words and/or numbers to compare the amount of carbon dioxide released for each type of car. **The ratio in g/mile for the amount of carbon dioxide released is: 368 gasoline-powered: 205 hybrid: 100 electric**
2. Assume each car was driven 100 miles in a week. How much carbon dioxide would be released? **gasoline-powered = 36,800 grams; hybrid = 20,500 grams; electric = 10,000 grams**
   As each car type drives more miles, how significant is the difference in the amount of carbon dioxide released for each type? **The more that a car is driven, the more significant the amount of greenhouse gases the car emits is.**
3. How would the amount of carbon dioxide released change for the electric car if all the electricity came from alternative energy sources? **The amount of carbon dioxide released would be 0 g/mile.**

Page 60: Food Has a Carbon Footprint: Field Trip to the Grocery Store: **Answers will vary.**

Page 63: Why Recycle - **The coloring is not done for the answer key.**

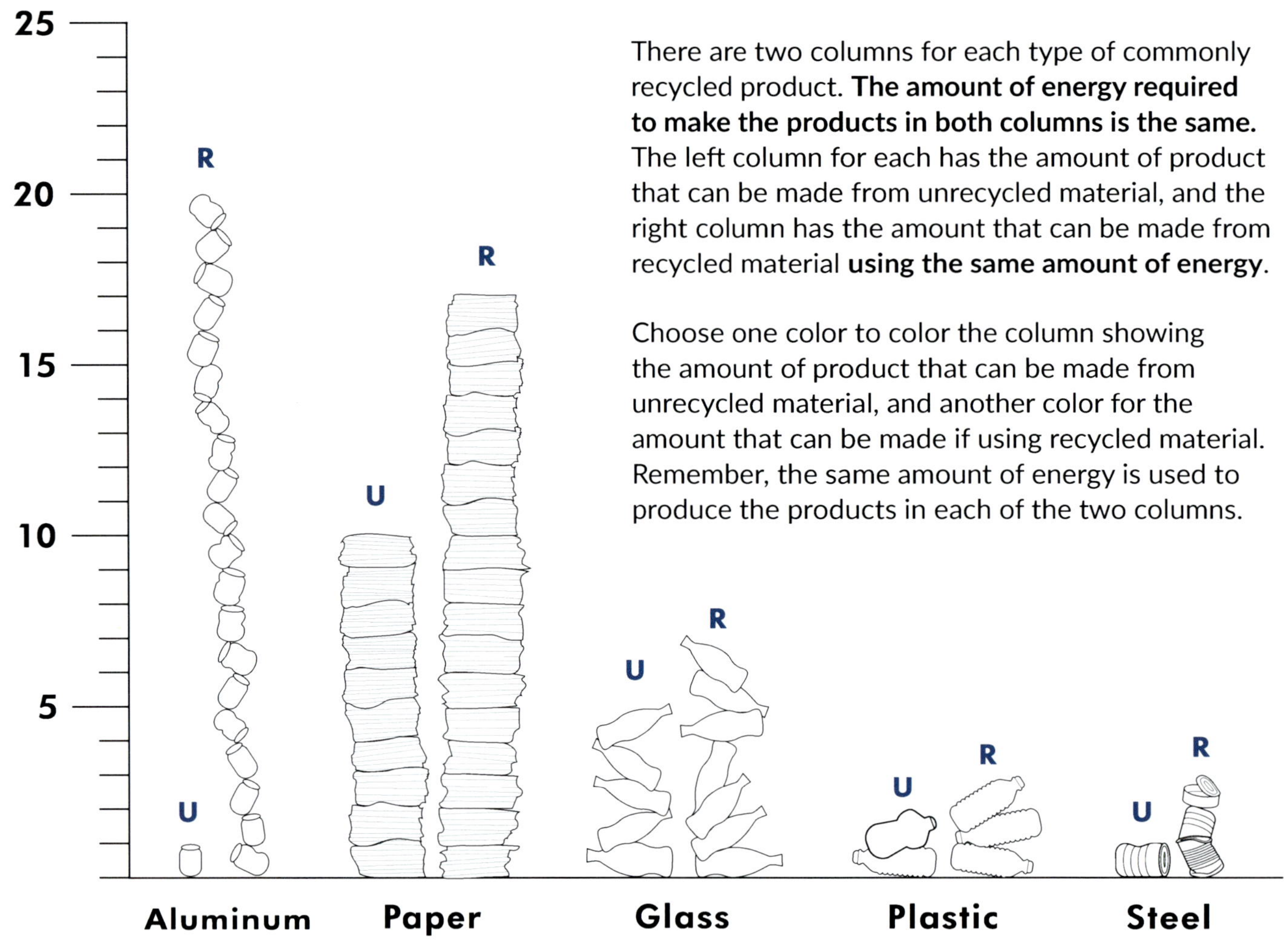

Aluminum		Paper		Glass		Plastic		Steel	
UNRECYCLED	RECYCLED	UNRECYCLED	RECYCLED	UNRECYCLED	RECYCLED	UNRECYCLED	RECYCLED	UNRECYCLED	RECYCLED
1	20	10	17	5	7	2	3	1	3

Using the same amount of energy, how many new aluminum cans can be made from unrecycled versus recycled aluminum? **1 from unrecycled materials vs 20 from recycled materials**

Using the same amount of energy, how much new paper can be made from unrecycled versus recycled paper? **10 from unrecycled materials vs 17 from recycled materials**

Using the same amount of energy, how much new glass can be made from unrecycled versus recycled glass? **5 from unrecycled materials vs 7 from recycled materials**

Using the same amount of energy, how much new plastic can be made from unrecycled versus recycled plastic? **2 from unrecycled materials vs 3 from recycled materials**

Using the same amount of energy, how many new steel cans can be made from unrecycled versus recycled steel cans? **1 from unrecycled materials vs 3 from recycled materials**

Which type of material saves the most energy to recycle? Circle the correct answer. **Aluminum**

In one to two sentences explain how recycling saves energy. **More of the same goods can be made using the same amount of energy if starting with recycled versus unrecycled materials**

In one to two sentences explain the benefits of recycling instead of having materials go to dumps and landfills. **In addition to polluting land and water, decomposing materials at dumps and landfills emit greenhouse gases into the air.**

Page 65: How I Am Going to Shrink My Carbon Footprint and Help Stop Global Warming

Answers will vary.

GLOSSARY

Adapt: To adjust to changing condition.

Air: The invisible gas surrounding Earth made of nitrogen, oxygen, argon, carbon dioxide, neon, methane, nitrous oxide, and other gas molecules.

Argon: A type of atom and a type of gas molecule in air.

Atoms: The small particles that make molecules.

Bond: A link between atoms.

Composting: The process of allowing organic materials, like coffee grounds, banana peels, and eggshells, to decay to use as fertilizer.

Carbon dioxide: A type of gas molecule in air. Carbon dioxide is a greenhouse gas.

Carbon footprint: The amount of carbon dioxide and other carbon compounds emitted into the air because of energy consumption.

Carbon sink: Something that absorbs and stores more carbon dioxide from the atmosphere than it releases.

Centimeter: A measurement of distance. There are 2.54 centimeters in an inch.

Chemical reactions: Process by which the atoms in a molecule combine, separate, or rearrange to make a new and different molecule.

Climate: The temperature, rain and snowfall, and wind in an area measured using weather data collected over 30 or more years. Climate is a long-term measurement.

Concentration: A measure of the amount of something in a mixture.

Extinction: When all the members of a species die.

Feedback Mechanism: A loop system, where the occurrence of one thing leads to something else, which through one or more events causes the system to respond in the same direction (a positive feedback loop) or the opposite direction (a negative feedback loop).

Gas molecules: Tiny moving particles made of atoms. Air is made of gas molecules.

Global climate change: The climate change that is happening now over the entire planet.

Global warming: The increase in temperature that has occurred since the Industrial Revolution.

Globe: A rounded, spherical object.

Greenhouse Effect: The trapping of energy by greenhouse gases that is then released in the form of heat. This process warms the air.

Greenhouse gases: Gas molecules that absorb energy from the sun and radiate it as heat into the air, which heats the air. Carbon dioxide, methane, nitrous oxide, and water are greenhouse gases.

Hypothesis: A prediction based on observations. Its purpose is to be tested through experimentation.

Ice cores: Long cores from ice that formed over thousands of years containing air bubbles with air from the time period when the ice formed. Scientists use ice cores to analyze the air from the time it was laid down.

Industrial Revolution: The period that began over 200 years ago when machines were invented that produced electricity. Those machines replaced animals and humans as a source of power. The machines invented during the Industrial Revolution use coal, gasoline, and oil to make the electricity needed to power them.

Landfill: Where trash is disposed of after it leaves your house.

Meteorologists: People who study and make predictions about the weather.

Methane: A type of gas molecule in air. Methane is a greenhouse gas.

Molecule: The tiny particles that make all matter, including air.

Neon: A type of atom and a type of gas molecule in the air.

Nitrogen: A type of atom that bonds in pairs to form the most common type of gas molecule in air.

Nitrous oxide: A type of gas molecule in air. Nitrous oxide is a greenhouse gas.

Observation: Careful study.

Organisms: Living beings.

Outgassing: The escape of gas from volcanoes.

Oxygen: A type of atom that bonds in pairs to form the second most common type of gas molecule in the air.

Precipitation: Rain and snowfall.

Periodic Table: A table that lists the 118 different types of atoms in an orderly fashion based on the properties of the atoms.

Radiate: To give off, to emit.

Rate: The speed at which something happens or moves.

Scientific method: An approach that uses a six-step process relying on logic to ask and answer questions.

Species: Living beings that can produce offspring that can then produce their own offspring.

Water vapor: Water molecules in the gas state.

Weather: The temperature, rain and snowfall, and wind in an area measured in hours and days. Weather is a short-term measurement.